got the life

got the life

My journey of Addiction, Faith, Recovery, and Korn

FIELDY

WITH LAURA MORTON

wm

WILLIAM MORROW
An Imprint of HarperCollinsPublishers

HarperCollins books may be purchased for educational, business, or sales promotional use. For information please write: Special Markets Department, HarperCollins Publishers, 10 East 53rd Street, New York, NY 10022.

FIRST EDITION

Designed by Renato Stanisic

Library of Congress Cataloging-in-Publication Data

Fieldy, 1969–
    Got the life : my journey of addiction, faith, recovery, and Korn / Fieldy with Laura Morton. — 1st ed.
       p. cm.
    ISBN 978-0-06-166249-2
    1. Fieldy, 1969– 2. Rock musicians—United States— Biography. I. Morton, Laura, 1964– II. Title.

ML420.F465A3 2009
782.42166092—dc22
[B]   2008037087

09 10 11 12 13 OV/RRD 10 9 8 7 6 5 4 3 2 1

TO MY DAD, REGINALD ARVIZU

Enter through the
narrow gate. For wide is the
gate and broad is the road
that leads to destruction,
and many enter through it.
But small is the gate and
narrow is the road that leads
to life and few will find it.

MATTHEW 7:13–14
(Today's New International Version)

CONTENTS

FALLING AWAY FROM ME

I was on tour in 2008 when I found myself checking into a hotel in London where the band usually stayed when we were there. When I checked in, I was taken to a room I hadn't thought about for years. The second the porter opened the door, the memories of one particularly horrible night came flooding back. I had stayed in that room before. Up until that moment, I hadn't remembered much of what happened that fateful night. And now, I couldn't get the visions out of my mind. I was having a flashback. . . . I had attacked Dena in this very room.

The porter could see I was having some type of reaction. He assumed the room wasn't to my liking. The room was fine. It was thoughts of my former self I was having problems with.

That night in London a few years back started out like any other normal evening. I met the guys in the band at Nobu, a restaurant in the hotel we were staying at while touring Europe. We sat at a large round table in the back slamming

When he filled in for David on drums, I surprised Joey Jordison by wearing his signature Kabuki-style mask onstage, 2007.

back sake and beer, eating sushi and getting drunk. Dena might have had a beer or two that night, but she knew I didn't like her drinking like the rest of us. As the night went on, I noticed one of the guys at the table was sitting a little too close to Dena. He spent a good part of the night whispering in her ear, which made her laugh that girly come-on laugh. I thought she was flirting with him. By this point in the evening, my perspective was anything but clear. I was completely in the bag, which blurred my judgment about as much as my vision. Maybe I was just being paranoid and drunk. But then, I saw the guy give Dena a kiss on the cheek.

"We're going to bed," I announced as I grabbed Dena's arm to pull her up from the table. "Now!" I was quickly boiling over with pure rage.

Dena had no idea why I was so angry. I wouldn't say a word to her when she pleaded to know what was happening. Silence was my usual way of handling these types of situations.

When we got up to the room, I began pushing and shoving Dena around like a rag doll, yelling and calling her a whore. I cornered Dena in the bathroom, where I pushed her so hard she fell into the tub. She was screaming and crying, wanting to know what she had done to make me so angry. I kept telling her to shut up. I didn't want to hear her cries or excuses. I finally beat her down to the bathroom floor before I stopped. I got up for a moment, and when I did, she was somehow able to shove me out the door and lock herself in.

I yelled, "I'm out of here!"

I pretended to walk out of the hotel room, letting the door slam shut, but I didn't go anywhere.

I couldn't hear a sound coming from the bathroom where Dena had locked herself in. I wasn't sure if she was passed out or just stunned into silence.

I decided to charge the door to break it down like they do in the movies.

That was a mistake.

The door was really thick. All I did was crush my shoulder, but I was too drunk to feel any pain until the next day. Eventually, I tired myself out. I was eerily calm when I told Dena that now I was really leaving.

But, again, I didn't go anywhere.

I crouched down a few feet away and, like a hunter patiently awaiting my prey, waited for her to open the door. Twenty minutes must have passed before I heard the first sound come from inside the bathroom. I could see the shadow of her feet at the bottom of the door. I heard Dena unlatch the lock. Boom. This was the moment I was waiting for.

When she opened the door, I rushed into the bathroom, grabbed Dena, and threw her down hard onto the bed. I was shoving and kicking her until she could no longer fight back. I took a pillow and crammed it over her face. I wrapped my other hand around her neck so she couldn't breathe. Her body flailed about, convulsing from side to side. She was helpless and scared.

Something had taken control of me—I didn't even know what I was doing. When her body stopped convulsing, I realized what had just happened. *Oh my God,* I thought. *I killed her.* I let go of my choke hold and pushed myself back. Dena began to cry. I was relieved she wasn't dead.

But me? I had to be dying inside to do something like that to someone I supposedly loved. How could I get to a point like this? Read on.

OLD FIELDY'S RULES

I was an expert at drinking, smoking dope, popping pills, using foul language, being mean, and partying without any remorse. You don't get that good at anything without lots of practice. Over time, I formed my own set of twisted rules:

1. *No morals necessary*
2. *Responsibility for any act not required*
3. *No act was wrong or immoral*
4. *Nothing was out of bounds*
5. *Faith in a higher being was nonexistent*
6. *The world revolved around me*
7. *The more women, drugs, and booze, the better*

These were the rules of the Old Fieldy. The rules of destruction. I was a rock star, living the life. These excessive compulsions turned me into a selfish, mean, and out-of-control jerk.

CHAPTER 1

ALL IN THE FAMILY

I've been clean for three years. I don't fight with my wife anymore. I don't lust or cheat anymore. I don't overeat before I go to bed anymore. I don't have to try and remember anything I did because I don't lie anymore. I don't hate to come home anymore. I don't put off my dreams anymore. I don't wake up feeling like hell anymore. I don't spend money on things I later regret anymore. I don't deny my blessed life that has been waiting for me . . . anymore.

I began sending my friends and family text messages like the one above shortly after my father died in 2005. Losing Dad was my wake-up call to see that I had to change the way I lived or I was going to die, too.

By the time my father fell ill, he had become a total Holy Roller, completely into Jesus. But he never once made me feel like the way I was living was wrong—even when he knew I had fallen pretty far off the right track. I had spent the last twenty years of my life popping pills, drinking beer, smoking weed, and throwing wild parties at my house. I was living the life I thought I was supposed to be living as a rock star. Dad often came to visit and hang out, but he never once said a negative word or made me feel judged for my actions. You'd never know Dad was a religious man because he loved hanging and having a good time, something he could easily do sober. Of course, he wasn't always that way and that's why I thought having a good time was all about getting drunk or being high. I was oblivious that I was on a path of destruction.

Long before I was born, Dad made his living as a musician. He was in a band called Reggie and Alex—Dad being the "Reggie" in the name. They were one of the hottest bands around, packing in sold-out venues all throughout Southern California. He played guitar, the bass pedals, and keyboard and sang while Alex played drums. Dad was an extremely talented and gifted musician.

We shared a common bond from the day I was born—literally—which was our love of music. I was born in Los Angeles in 1969. Back in the day, Mom traveled with Dad and the band all the time. But, the stress and transient lifestyle of being on the road became too hard for her toward the end of her pregnancy so she just stayed at home until the big day. When she went into labor, every musician Dad knew in L.A. came to the hospital to support my parents as they welcomed their only son on November 2.

Six weeks later, our family was back on the road, traveling in Dad's white tricked-out van so Reggie and Alex could finish the last leg of their tour. Our first stop was Aspen. The band set up while I slept onstage in my infant seat. Touring with the band didn't last too long, however, because my parents realized the road wasn't the right place to raise a kid. Since they made the choice to start a family, Dad would have to make the necessary sacrifices to ensure I had a good stable life.

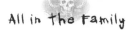
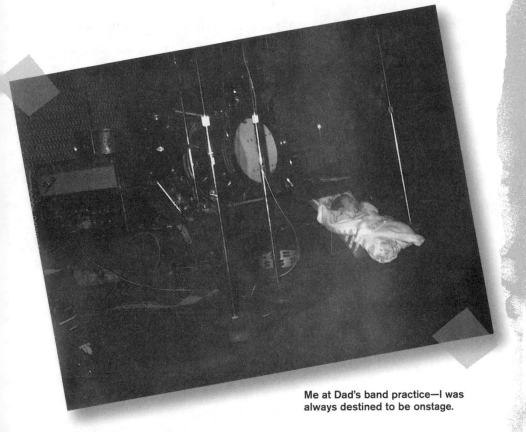

Me at Dad's band practice—I was always destined to be onstage.

By the time I was around three or four years old, my family was living in Bakersfield. We moved into our first house that was literally in the 'hood. We were the only white family on our street. I vividly remember the day we moved in because I never thought I was "white" until I took a good look around the neighborhood, which was primarily black and Hispanic. My father's family heritage is Spanish Basque, so I have very dark features. If I had to, I could easily pass for Mexican.

I got my looks from my dad. His complexion was so dark that he looked half black and half Mexican. He had black curly hair that he'd blow-dry straight, so it looked longer. When he didn't blow-dry his hair, it was more of an Afro.

He had a big thick handlebar mustache that made him look extremely ethnic.

Dad was the epitome of 1970s cool. He wore button-up T-shirts with funky designs on them, shirts with big wide collars, opened halfway down his chest, and those crazy 1970s platform boots with a zipper on the side. He was always dressed in style—or at least what *he* thought was in style. I'd look at him and think, "I'm never dressing like that!" But that was hip at the time, so to the rest of the world, he looked cool.

On the day we moved into our new home, neighbors stood outside their homes, staring at us as my folks tried to get us settled in. When I woke up the next morning, I looked out my bedroom window to see if all of those strange faces were still there. That's when I noticed our house and Dad's brand-new truck had been egged the night before. I was really scared. I didn't want to live there. I had never experienced racism or prejudice, and my mind was too young to understand why anyone would want to hurt us.

When Dad woke up that same morning, he told me I had to go out and make friends with the other kids, but I didn't want to hang out with anyone in that neighborhood. I would have been very content staying inside forever. I was a pretty shy kid anyway, so making friends was hard enough. Trying to fit in as the only white boy in a neighborhood of Hispanics and blacks scared me to death. Dad told me I could say I was Mexican or white—whichever I wanted. Maybe he was joking, but at the time, I felt confused. Even though I looked it, I wasn't Mexican at all. I reluctantly took his advice and did what I had to do so I wouldn't get beat up.

Reggie and Alex continued to play gigs primarily in Bakersfield for most of my childhood. By the time I was eight or nine, Dad would sometimes let me come to a sound check at whatever club they were playing. I'd sit at the bar drinking a Coke with a cherry in it, pretending I was older and enjoying an alcoholic drink. I thought it was awesome to hang out at the bar like I was one of the guys.

I know that most kids think their dad is the coolest dude, but to me, my dad was the real deal because he played in a band. I grew up spending many nights watching Dad play, learning from him, and wanting to be just like him. The band often kicked it in our garage, jamming out 1970s rock-and-roll tunes with an edge. Their playlist ranged from Eric Clapton's "Cocaine" to anything by Led Zeppelin. Their music choices influenced my own tastes, which were as varied as theirs. I always had my stereo blaring when I was a kid. I had a love for all types of music.

For most of their marriage, my mother was pretty much a stay-at-home mom. She was a typical suburban housewife with blond hair and an innocence that made her appear soft and not edgy at all. She was really skinny, always wore hot pants and big oversized sunglasses, and was definitely sexier than all the other moms. As a kid, I didn't want my mom to look sexy. I wanted her to look more conservative, like everyone else's mom. Maybe Mom thought she had to dress like a diva because Dad was a musician. It was clear that she wanted to stay young and attractive. My sisters and I were kind of embarrassed by her appearance and often pleaded with her to dress more her age. Looking back, she was young and probably very appropriate, but at the time it seemed too over the top.

To make some extra money, Mom started a babysitting service, sometimes taking in as many as ten or fifteen kids during the day. Her home business started out by watching some of the kids from the guys in Dad's band during practices. One of those kids included Jonathan Davis, whose father was now with Dad's band. Mom's business quickly rolled into more and more kids being dropped off during the day. She was really good with kids. She liked having them around, and it was a pretty lucrative way for her to earn some extra money without having to work outside the home.

I have three sisters—Candi, who is seven years older than me and has a different dad; Mandi, who is seven years younger than me; and Robin, who is slightly younger than Mandi. Our life was one big party growing up. There were always people at our house, partying, playing music, and having a good time. Reggie and Alex had broken up, but Dad kept right on playing music with another group of guys. The wives and girlfriends all hung out while the band jammed. I

With my older sister, Candi.

spent countless nights sitting in the garage on an opened-up lawn chair listening to their music, carefully watching as I daydreamed about someday becoming a big rock star. That's where it all started for me.

Dad kept a refrigerator in the garage that was always stocked full of Budweiser. He'd often ask me to grab him a beer. I thought it was cool to hang out and pop open beers for the guys. Eventually I began taking tiny sips off the top of a freshly cracked can before handing it over. A sip here and there quickly turned into a lot more drinking than a twelve-year-old boy should be doing. I watched the guys get tanked and thought *that* is what you're *supposed* to do when you play in a band. I didn't know any better—like any kid, I just wanted to be like my dad. Eventually, I began sneaking beers out of the garage and into my room until I had four or more hidden under my bed. I drank them warm, until I could feel the buzz—which I liked, so I kept drinking more.

I liked the way drinking alcohol made me feel. It didn't take long to start pinching Mom's Bartles and James California Coolers, too. Looking back, they were nasty, but at the time they got me *really* drunk, *really* fast. It wasn't unusual for me to drink by myself either. I saw Mom drink alone plenty of times. I thought that was normal. Unfortunately, I was too young to realize there are limits. I didn't know when to stop, so I usually drank until I got sick. I vividly remember throwing up from drinking too many coolers one night. Chunks of half-digested hot dogs I ate for dinner got stuck in my throat. It took me a while to eat hot dogs again after that—but I was right back to drinking the very next day.

Even though the parties were always fun around the house, too much drinking usually resulted in some type of altercation between Mom and Dad toward the end of the night. There

That's me, Little Fieldog, out in the dirt fields where my family spent a lot of time riding dirt bikes.

were many evenings they got into a quarrel, and sometimes an all-out brawl. I vividly recall hearing my mother scream out to me one night when I was around eight years old. She was yelling that my father was trying to kill her.

"Reggie, Reggie. Come get me. Help me! He's killing me!" I could hear my mother pleading for my help. I didn't want to hear her shrieks of terror, but she kept calling for me to come help until I could no longer ignore her cries. When I walked into the living room, I saw Dad on top of Mom, choking her.

They were screaming at each other until I finally yelled back, "Get off her!" I pushed Dad, my hero, until he let go. After I pushed him off, Dad took a step back, looked right at me, glanced at Mom, who was crying and lying on the ground and then he just walked away without saying a word. I was scared and confused. I began to cry as my mother scooped me up and held me for what seemed like hours. It took me a while to finally catch my breath. We never spoke about that night, though it left a pretty vivid impression on me.

I had really severe seasonal allergies when I was a kid. I always had a very hard time breathing, but they got especially bad during allergy season. My nickname at home was "Squeaky" because my voice made squeaky noises from being so congested all the time. Not long after that incident between Mom and Dad, I noticed I was having an unusually hard time breathing one night. Even though I suffered from chronic allergies, I wasn't the type of kid who ever complained. But on this particular night, my breathing was really shallow and I was short of breath. When I walked into my parents' room to tell them something was wrong, Dad blew off what I was saying and told me to go back to bed. Thankfully, my mother realized it wasn't normal for me to complain so she came into my room a minute later to check on me. That's when she realized something was very wrong. Mom rushed me to the hospital where the doctors told her I had a severe case of pneumonia. They said my lungs had filled with fluid and that I could have died if the infection had been left to fester much longer. The doctor insisted that I be admitted right away. I spent the next two weeks recovering.

While I was there, my two younger sisters were also admitted to the same hospital. They had gotten into the medicine cabinet and eaten an entire bottle of Flintstone vitamins and were suffering from horrible stomach pain from the overdose.

Although I didn't know it at the time, my parents didn't

have health insurance. Having three kids in the hospital at the same time nearly bankrupted our family. Dad was forced to sell our house and get a job cleaning carpets during the day to supplement his income from playing music. He had a friend who helped him start his own small business by financing his first truck. Once he got the company going, he was able to buy another small home that was right next to the local railroad tracks. The entire house would shake whenever a train rumbled by.

Dad's carpet cleaning service kept him busy during the days. Sometimes, whenever I could, I'd tag along to help out, learning the business—and other habits—from Dad at an early age. He was always checking out young girls as we'd ride along in his truck. He'd make some comments about their bodies and stuff like that. His remarks weren't very nice, but I didn't think much of it. That was just my dad. He would try to spot women and skirts getting into their cars, making a game out of it. He'd say, "Let's try and get a leg shot," but I was too young to say anything.

I kept thinking, *What about Mom?*

I knew what he was doing was wrong, but it never seemed to lead to anything more than some harmless flirtation so I just rolled with it. I liked hanging with Dad too much to make an issue out of his behavior. Little did I know that his lack of respect for women would greatly influence my own relationships as I got older.

I heard my parents say they loved each other often, but the screaming, yelling, and wrong tone of voice drowned out the laughter and good times that seemed to come right before the heavy drinking began each night. During the day, everything was cool, but by early evening, everything changed. In the midst of their most heated arguments, something always ended up airborne. I remember one particular night when Mom began throwing the dinner plates at Dad. He ducked as they smashed against our old Kenmore refrigerator. The fights always seemed to start out as fun and games, but they quickly turned into violence and pure hatred. I'd sit back and watch the events unfold—certain of the direction things would go—and think to myself, *This is crazy.*

The violence at home always came at night. Sometimes Dad would smash food in Mom's face like it was funny; other times they'd get physical, pushing and shoving each other until it became a real fight. The altercations weren't always contained between Mom and Dad. One night Dad pointed to a small piece of food on the dinner table and told me to look at it. When I bent down, he said, "get closer." I had inched my way slightly closer when I felt my father's huge hand against the back of my head as he smashed my face into the scrap of food on the table, breaking my nose. I didn't want Dad to know how much it hurt, but I was in a lot of pain. Since I was too embarrassed to say anything, I never went to the hospital to have it checked out.

That type of behavior confused me because Dad was so cool during the daytime. I don't think Dad ever knew how hurtful he was being because he wasn't in his right mind. Whenever you drink a lot, your perception is distorted and what you think is funny is really hurtful. I didn't make the connection that his drinking was usually what sparked his uncontrollable rage until I was much older.

Looking back, I think I was such a quiet kid because I also grew up in a house filled with women who constantly bickered. I never felt right being in the fray as I watched my sisters argue with one another or with Mom. Candi and Mom used to get into some really heated arguments. Sometimes they would actually get physical too, hitting each other and pulling each other's hair. Their fights during Candi's teenage years made me grow thankful for the sound of the rumbling train that passed outside my window every ten minutes so I didn't have listen to their arguments. The train was loud enough to drown out all of the sounds I didn't want to hear inside my home.

The older I got, the more I realized there was never peace in that house. There was no peace but that's not to say there was absolutely no love in my parents' home. Sadly, though, there was a lot more violence than warmth or affection among all of us. My younger sisters and I were just trying to survive the uncertainty in our home.

As the only boy, Mom pretty much let me get away with everything. If I wanted to go somewhere, all it took was a hug and a puppy dog look and Mom gave me whatever I wanted. And I knew just how to butter her up. To this day she still has a hard time saying no to me if I lay it on thick enough.

By the time I was twelve, I had started getting into riding motorcycles, especially motocross and racing on tracks. Even though Mom thought it was dangerous, she supported my passion. I'd take my dirt bike out and ride until the sun went down—partly because I loved being on my bike and partly because I didn't want to be around the mounting violence at home.

Rick Davis and my dad also loved to go riding on weekends, so sometimes we'd all ride together. That's what families like ours did in Bakersfield on the weekend—we rode three-wheelers and dirt bikes. One weekend Jonathan came with us. He was a pretty mellow kid while I had turned into a bit of a punk and a bully. Jon was kind of a nerd when he was younger. He wore his hair short all over except his bangs,

Racing around on my first minibike, age six.

which were long and feathered. He always had a certain edge to his nerdiness, often wearing Marshall T-shirts, and he had an innate rock-and-roll style. Even though we weren't really friends when we were kids, we were often forced to hang out together. I was such a mean kid that I would usually spend those days constantly picking on Jon.

On one particular day, Jon and I were out trying to climb the steep dirt hills on our three-wheelers.

I kept taunting Jon to "go climb the hill."

He was so scared.

The second he showed his vulnerability, I immediately jumped all over the opportunity to razz him.

"You sissy," I said. "Go climb that hill, you chicken." He didn't budge, so I jumped on my three-wheeler, hit the gas, and "accidentally" ran him over. I didn't care. I just kept right on going until I reached the top of the hill. I didn't really hit him on purpose, but I can't say it was a complete accident, either. I was indifferent and never looked back after I realized what had happened. All I cared about was getting to the top. Even though he didn't get hurt, unless you count his pride, he never got over the trauma. He still reminds me of that story from time to time. So here it is. . . . Jon, if you're reading this, I will lie on the ground for you anytime and let you run me over with a three-wheeler so we can call it even! (Let me also say this: if you think running over a friend is cool, think again. I was young and stupid and I would never do something like that today, so don't try this at home.)

I was becoming really good at motorcycle riding, competing in races all over California. I loved going fast. I had ab-

Around my house it was dirt bikes and rock and roll. Age six.

solutely no fear. My old bike wasn't fast enough anymore, so I finally got the bike of my dreams . . . a brand-new Kawasaki KX80. It was dark green and faster than any other bike on the course. Nobody else had one so I thought I was the coolest kid out there. I could take it on the straightaway and beat everyone. I wanted to turn pro and this bike was my ticket.

Then, two of my friends, Geno and Troy, ended up getting the same bike I had. I thought it was cool we all had the same machine until I realized they were better racers than me. Up until that point, I had the fastest bike on the track. It didn't matter if I wasn't quite as skilled as they were because I would win all of the races. Once the three of us got on the track riding the same bikes, though, they left me in the dust. In fact, I was so lame, it was all I could do to make sure they didn't lap me!

From that day on I realized there would always be people in the world who were better than me. There was no way I would ever get as good as they were because I didn't race often enough. I thought about that for days until it occurred to me that becoming a rock star was my true passion, anyway. Motorcycles were just a hobby, so I focused on learning how to play the guitar. I practiced for hours, teaching myself chords and riffs. Dad showed me some of the basics so I sort of knew what I was doing, but I didn't take to it right away.

What really motivated me to get serious about the guitar was my last ride on a three-wheeler. My older sister, Candi, and I had gone out for a ride. She kept telling me to put on my helmet but I didn't want to. She said I couldn't ride unless I did, so I finally gave in. Good thing I did. I took off and hit a huge bump. I flipped over the handlebars and landed in front of the three-wheeler just in time to have it run over me. It dragged me underneath for several yards. When the machine finally came to a stop, I had broken my arm and smashed my left pinky finger, which was so swelled, it looked more like a big toe! Thank God my sister begged me to wear that helmet. It had deep gashes on the top, which confirmed to me I could have died without it.

My arm and hand injuries were so bad I was worried I might not be able to continue playing guitar. I also remember screaming in pain and fear that I would be disfigured and that girls wouldn't like me. I was inconsolable on the way to the hospital. I swore I'd never get on another motorcycle if God would let me heal from the crash.

It took about a year or so to completely heal. During that time I concentrated on trying to rehabilitate my arm and pinky by playing the guitar for hours every day. I was never without that thing strapped to my back. Dad taught me the proper way to play and read every type of music, from classical to classic rock. It was really hard, but I forced myself to do it because I knew being a musician would someday be the way I made a living.

Every now and then, I'd ask Dad to show me how to play a particular song, whether he knew it or not. He had such a perfect ear that he could sit down and just play whatever I requested. I was blown away that Dad could just figure out a song by listening to it. I was really into Queensrÿche at the time, and miraculously, Dad could play any of their songs by ear without ever having played them before. That's talent.

By the time I started at Compton Junior High I knew I wanted to be in a band. There were two other guys at my school who were the only other music dudes around. Brian "Head" Welch, who got his nickname way back in junior high because of the size of his head and James "Munky" Shaffer, whose nickname came a few years later because of his

I'm fifteen, and in the early days of guitar before I discovered bass.

feet. (Munky could grab stuff with his toes!) The three of us quickly became friends. We were totally into the heavy metal sound, listening to bands like Dio and Iron Maiden. Head sported crop top hair that he was desperate to grow out. We wore skintight straight-leg jeans with bandannas tied around our legs and leather vests so we would look like musicians.

Even though they were young, those guys were already really good guitarists. They could play so much better than I could. The pressure was on to keep practicing if I was ever going to be as good as they were. I tried hard, but I never seemed to be good enough. Playing the guitar just wasn't natural to me.

On the other hand, Head was naturally gifted. He was an amazing guitarist. I never met anyone who could play like he did. He played solos and every great rock tune imaginable.

When he played Ozzy solos, I'd watch in complete awe. He made it look easy—which it is not. To me, he was the ultimate guitar player.

Head and I talked about everything from music to our fathers. He told me about his dad, who Head said was an alcoholic. I didn't know it at the time, but I could have probably said the same about my dad, too.

I'd often go to Head's house to hang out in his basement, where we'd sneak his dad's alcohol. Our sole goal was to get wasted.

One afternoon his father came home early and busted us. We were drunk and being stupid, laughing and making jokes as his dad came into the basement. Head's dad yelled at him like I had never heard a father yell before. Dad had a bad temper, to be sure, but I don't recall ever feeling as scared as I did that day in Head's basement. My nervousness gave way to unexpected and uncontrollable laughter as Head's dad went off on us. I was drunk and scared. The harder I tried to contain my laughing, the worse it got. When he was done yelling at Head, his father turned toward me, pointed his finger right in my face, and said, "And you're a jerk too, Reggie!" Head and I both laughed for an hour after he went upstairs. Life was pretty good. I had some cool friends, was learning to play music, and thought everything was going along fine.

My world came suddenly crashing down on my first day of high school. A large moving van was waiting in front of our house when I came home from school. Dad came outside to tell me Mom was moving out and they were getting a divorce. I knew they didn't have the perfect marriage, but I was truly shocked by the revelation that it was over. I had grown so accustomed to the violence and screaming, I just thought that was their way of loving each other. I didn't have a real emotional reaction. No tears or visible signs that I was upset. At the time, I'm not sure I even knew how to show my feelings, but I was torn apart on the inside.

Dad went on to tell me that I was going to live with him.

He said, "We boys . . . us men . . . we've got to stick together." Men? I was only fourteen years old. When I asked about my sisters, Dad said they were going to live with Mom, though he reassured me that I could visit Mom whenever I wanted.

I thought, *That's cool.*

I told Dad he didn't need to be sad. In fact, I suggested we throw a party. I got some of my friends together, Dad got a keg, and we partied in our big empty house the night Mom moved out. Dad's band played while my friends, Dad, his buddies, and me all got drunk. A kegger sounded like the perfect solution to our broken hearts.

I often think back on that day because that was the first time I ever felt like I had a broken heart. Those emotions were difficult for me to handle. From that day forward, I protected my heart from ever being hurt again. Though it wouldn't be a conscious decision, I would never allow anyone to get close enough to me for fear of feeling that type of pain.

Eventually, Dad and I moved into a small apartment together. Now that I was older, he was back on the road, touring with the band. I was alone a lot. With no one looking over my shoulder, I could have parties whenever I wanted. Dad didn't mind. He'd come home after playing a gig and party with my friends and me like he was one of the guys. He'd drink with us and have a really good time.

By now, Head and I were really good friends. One day he turned to me and said, "Man, I want to start a band but—I need a bass player."

Playing in one of my early high school bands at the
Kern County Fair.

Even though I was just starting out, I knew I wanted to play
in a band with Head. I didn't care if I had to play the bass, the
maracas, or crash a couple of cymbals. I was more than happy
to learn the bass if it meant playing in my own band. I never
admitted to Head that I wasn't very good and Head never said
that he already knew I sucked. Head offered to show me a
couple of bass lines to help me transition from the guitar.

I worked all summer long to save up enough money to buy
my first bass. It was an Ibanez, the same brand I use today. I
worked the worst job I've ever had that summer to pay for the
guitar, building swimming pools for a local company in Bakersfield. They didn't even have a tractor so we had to hand

shovel the dirt and use a wheelbarrow to dump the debris. It was brutal being in the hot sun all day digging those holes, but worth it to pay for my bass.

To make some more money, I also worked for a company that cleaned burlap bags. Their offices were in Cottonwood, the worst part of Bakersfield. It was straight ghetto. My friend Kip and I were the only two white guys there. It was just the gangstas and us.

The job consisted of a bunch of guys cleaning and folding bags in a shed that felt like it was around 120 degrees inside. There was a huge vent at the top of the shed that we'd push the bags into, which would then suck the dirt and dust out. We had to wear masks because the debris was horrible to breathe in. I hated that job, but I knew I had to save up money so I kept doing it until I finally had enough to quit and get the bass I wanted.

I practiced playing bass even more than I did the guitar. It felt far more natural to me. I could be more aggressive and began developing my signature style of playing. I found I could hold the bass upright and slap away at it really hard. I loved the feeling of banging it like a big toy. I was ready for stardom.

Head and I asked our friends, John Charles and Ron French, to be our drummer and the lead singer. We called ourselves Pierced. Back then, Head wrote all of the music and lyrics. He wrote some pretty funny songs like "Bad, Bad Girls" and "Fantasy Lover." They were sort of glam rock songs. I mostly listened to Mötley Crüe, TNT, King Cobra and Icon, wanting so much to be just like those guys. Our band was a blend of all of their sounds. I didn't care what we played. I was simply psyched to be in the band. I was happy to let Head tell us what to do so I could just play.

It was around this time I got the nickname "Fieldy," which everybody asks me about. It's unusual, so I can understand why so many people are curious to know its roots. The name evolved from my early days in Pierced. All of us spent long afternoons in John's garage jamming, drinking beer, and joking around. I had kind of a chubby face back then, so it wasn't long before John started calling me "Gopher."

"Man, it looks like you're storing food in your cheeks," Johnny said.

Head and John laughed hysterically every time one of them said it, but I didn't mind. I thought it was kind of funny, too. In fact, everyone got a kick out of my new nickname. It became sort of an inside joke between my friends and me at school. Whenever there was a big group of people around, someone would say it to me under their breath and a few of us would bust out laughing. If someone muttered "Gopher," it was garbled and came out sounding more like "Gar." Oddly enough, the new version of the name caught on and before I knew it, everyone started calling me "Gar."

For whatever reason, Gar quickly evolved into "Gar*field*" and when people grew tired of that, they got rid of the first half of the word and began calling me "Field." Eventually, we added a "y" to the end, and people have been calling me Fieldy ever since.

Pierced was becoming pretty popular. I loved every minute of being in that band. Even though we were a bunch of sixteen-year-old kids, it didn't take long for us to find a manager who believed in us. His name was Clyde. He was a local doctor who wasn't really a music manager, but he had seen us play at a local club and liked us enough to put us on a salary for around a hundred bucks a week. He even paid for all of our equipment and studio costs. I couldn't believe I was actually getting paid to do what I loved. I would have done it for free. But I was happy to have the money. I had odd jobs all throughout high school, but music was my true passion. Though I still made some extra money cleaning carpets with Dad from time to time, it wasn't nearly as much fun as playing in the band.

Clyde rented a local club for us to use as rehearsal space called the Royal Palms. We thought we were on top of the world. We had a manager, a huge place to practice in, and . . . we were actually getting paid! We all tripped out over our good fortune. Once again, life was good.

Once I found my passion for music, education no longer had a lot of significance to me. Music was my life. I thought I didn't need school. I was going to be a rock star. I knew it, too. So I stopped learning. Worse yet, I began cheating. The only reason I didn't drop out of school was because Dad wouldn't let me. "You're finishing school!" That was all he would say, no matter what arguments I posed.

Eventually, I realized he was right. After a lifetime of going to school, I only had four years left. If I dropped out, that would have made all of those previous years a waste of time. Even so, I still pretty much gave up and skated by those last four years by cheating my way through. It became a game to me to see if I could get away with it. I looked over people's shoulders, stole ideas from other people's papers, and had someone else do my homework.

Of course, looking back, I completely regret my decision to give up on my education—especially my choice to cheat in English. That's the one subject everyone really needs. Now that I'm older, I realize there's so much I still have to learn. It sucks because if I had just paid attention, I wouldn't feel like I missed out on something that was so accessible. I knew what

got the life

Highland High School graduation—1988.

my dream was, but I wasn't smart enough to recognize that I could still have my dream *and* pursue my education. Well, there's not a lot I can do about it now except tell my story so others won't make the same mistakes.

Like Dad promised, I got to see Mom as much as I wanted to. I loved my mom so much. I didn't want to abandon her just because my parents got a divorce. When I was old enough to drive, Mom and her new husband, John, bought me a used Toyota pickup truck so I could go back and forth. I've always liked to drive pretty tricked-out cars, so that same year, they gave me really hot rims for Christmas. I bought a lowering kit from Pep Boys, and lowered the truck myself. I always liked working on cars, but this was different because now I was working on *my* car. I wanted it to be so cool.

I liked John. I think he started dating Mom shortly after my parents separated, and he was always respectful of my need to have one-on-one time with Mom. Whenever I'd come over, he made it a point to quietly slip out for a few hours so Mom and I could just hang out while she made a home-cooked meal for me—something I loved but rarely got at Dad's. Munky, Head, and some of my other friends loved Mom's cooking, so we'd inevitably end up at her house on weekends. We'd all come rolling in around five or six in the morning after a long night of partying to find her in the kitchen cooking breakfast before we went to bed.

Munky lived in Rosedale, about twenty minutes west of my house in Bakersfield. Even though it was on the complete opposite side of town, I didn't mind when I had to drive to his place to get him. I loved cruising in my pickup.

My first truck given to me by my stepdad before I put the rims on it. Man, I loved it.

I had gotten brand-new seventeen-inch chrome rims for my eighteenth birthday that I spent the whole day putting on my truck. Munky and I had plans to go out and celebrate my birthday. At the time, I had really long hair that I used to blow-dry upside down to get as much volume as I could. The bigger the better. I was wearing my peg pants, tight shirt, and even a little eyeliner to give me a *rocker* look. I always felt like the ultimate rock star guy when I got dressed for a night out.

Just before I left to pick up Munky, I noticed the left tail-light on my truck was broken. I ran into the garage to find something to fix it. The best I could come up with was a red rag, which I stuffed into the light. I figured that would get

Me with the amazing set of rims I got as a high school graduation present from my mom and stepdad.

me through the night. I climbed into the truck, cranked the stereo as loud as I could get it, rocked out to Icon, and headed out.

About ten minutes into the drive a car load of girls pulled up next to me. I purposely refused to give them the time of day. I thought I was too cool. I barely glanced over, as I drove with one hand on the wheel, nodding my head to the loud music. As I sped away, the girls came right up to me again, but this time they were screaming and yelling. Still, I gave them nothing. Finally, the third time they pulled up I decided to roll down the window.

"Hey, what's up?" I was being totally standoffish.

One of them yelled back, "Your car is on fire!" And then they drove off.

My face was as red as the rag in my taillight. I looked back in the rearview mirror and could see bright orange flames shooting up from the back of my car. I pulled over, got out, and kicked the rag until it fell to the ground. I was so embarrassed. Thankfully, there was no real damage done. Once I knew the fire was out, I climbed back into my truck and made my way to Munky's. When I told him what had happened, he just laughed.

By the time I was eighteen, I had begun partying all the time. I drank beer and had started to take speed pills. I was into Cross Tops and Magnums, which were good quality pills, but any type was fine. The first time I took a hit of speed was after I found a small black container in Dad's closet. He had a bunch of Tops. I didn't think it was a big deal since I knew Dad took them often. I thought that was what musicians did to keep up their energy and stamina. I would sneak a few here and there, certain Dad would never notice. I'm not sure he ever knew the

Easy to see why I won "Best Hair" in my senior yearbook.

truth, but even so, I don't think he would have cared. I eventually got hooked and had to start buying my own stash.

Image was everything to me as an aspiring rock icon. I wanted the big hair that was popular at the time, wore skin-tight jeans, and did my best to cultivate the bad boy image that went along with all of that. I became friends with a local hairstylist named Jan Mills, who was considered to be the best hairdresser in Bakersfield. She was a total rocker lady in her midthirties. If you had long hair, you went to see Jan. She used hot pink guitar picks with the phrase "Get your mop chopped by Jan Mills" as her business cards. I liked hanging out at her salon because there were always a lot of girls there, and Jan, who thought I looked a lot like her boyfriend, was always trying to hook me up. Even though dating was never a priority for me, I enjoyed the company of women a lot more than men. Most of my closest friends in school were girls. The only guys I hung out with were other musicians.

I never had a problem dating except I was never faithful. If a girl complained about my behavior, I'd always tell her to leave. None of them ever did. It was weird because the less affection I showed them, the more of my attention they wanted. My main focus was on my music and partying.

I wanted to be a rocker, to party, *and* to be skinny. Taking the speed was especially helpful to keep me skinny so I could wear my tight size 27 jeans and look the part of the skinny "rock star." Looking back, I looked too skinny. I was totally sucked up, but that was the look I was going for. I thought the pills were cool because not only was I not eating, I was getting

During my glam rock phase, 1986.

high. My heart raced and practically pounded through my chest. I thought that was the greatest feeling ever.

I didn't pay a lot of attention to that little voice inside my head that kept telling me I was messing up my life. I got so caught up in drinking and getting high that I ignored my inner soul. But sure enough, every night when I went to bed, I couldn't sleep. Partially because of the speed, but mostly because deep down, I knew what I was doing was wrong.

I did a lot of things that made me feel that way. I was cussing all of the time and began to steal—mostly candy bars and novelties like toys. Once I began drinking every single day, I always stole liquor because I wasn't old enough to buy it. I'm not sure if it was the rush or my lack of money. Either way, my need to steal was as out of control as my partying.

There was a place called the Fast Strip in Bakersfield that was like a 7-Eleven but it had a full deli counter where sandwiches were sold. I would always go in there with my friends. One of my buddies smoked, so he'd always walk up to the counter, ask for gum, and a pack of smokes. While the clerk turned his back to get the cigarettes, I'd grab a huge tub of beef jerky and hide it under my jacket. I usually had enough time to grab a couple of sandwiches and throw them on the floor by the front door so my buddy or I could kick them outside into the parking lot as we left the store. It was so easy, it became routine.

When petty thefts were no longer fulfilling, I wanted the rush of something bigger and more meaningful. I once plotted to rob the local 7-Eleven. I had it all figured out. I told my friend Kip that we could go into the store, spray paint over the security camera that watched every movement from high above, and hit the cash register. We could pretend we had guns by pointing our fingers through our coats. The plan was that I would snatch a bunch of candy bars as a distraction while Kip grabbed all of the money in the cash register before we made our getaway. I kept telling him how easy it would be and that we'd definitely get away with it. It was such stupid adolescent plotting, but it made so much sense to me at the time. Worse yet, once I plotted how to rob 7-Eleven, my thoughts turned toward bigger targets, such as our local bank. Luckily, we never went through with any of our "planned" heists, but those thoughts were always there.

By this time, I was hardly ever sober. The drunker I was, the better those crazy ideas sounded. Even so, I knew I was spending all of those sleepless nights making up lame excuses and fooling myself that I was acting appropriately. I had become a real punk. I didn't care about anyone else but myself. I would go into people's homes and trash them in a drunken rage. I couldn't have been more disrespectful—and these were often my friends' homes. I did whatever I wanted to do, from spitting to messing up their bathrooms and never saying a word that it was me. We were all so drunk and out of control, it could have been any one of us who did those things. In fact, it probably was all of us, which is why no one ever specifically called me out. By the time we all got together the next day, no one could remember who did what, so it seemed like a safe, albeit vicious cycle of violence and destruction.

My drinking was now a seven-day-a-week habit. I wasn't smoking pot yet, and since I have really bad allergies, snorting anything was pretty much out of the question unless I wanted to be miserable and in terrible pain. Believe it or not, I have never snorted anything. I probably would have if I could have, but it never made sense for me. My drugs of choice were alcohol, speed, and food. My speed habit had gotten so bad, that I would chop up speed pills until they were powder and down a fistful chased with an icy cold beer. The only time I ever tried crystal meth, I wrapped the rock up in a tiny piece of toilet paper and swallowed it. I was up for twenty-four hours straight. I tried to detail my pickup truck but it was a seemingly impossible task, like I had ADHD or something. I vigorously began sanding down the paint on the front bumper until it was half done and then began cleaning the inside of the truck with Q-tips. When morning came, I went inside the house and began to make breakfast for my friends who had stayed up all night to help me. I never wanted to be up that long. I just wanted to be skinny. Since the speed pills weren't really working for me anymore, I thought taking meth might help. I hated it.

By the end of high school I had put on a lot of weight. I was actually kind of heavy all throughout my later teenage years, which was so strange since I had spent most of my youth obsessing over being a skinny rocker. But all of my drinking and partying made that goal next to impossible because I began binge eating after long nights of boozing it up. I'd get drunk and then eat a bunch of really bad, greasy junk food right before I went to bed. Ultimately, it became my nightly routine to drink until I couldn't see, eat until I couldn't move, and then to simply pass out.

It had been years since I had a peaceful night's sleep. I spent most of the nights tossing and turning. I never realized why I was so miserable. I was filled with guilt. My brain didn't stand a chance of shutting down to allow me to sleep. I didn't know that I was feeling anxious. I chalked the sensation up to the effects of speed. In the end, my conscience never let me get away with my actions.

Mom could see I was partying a lot—too much. Eventually, I moved back home with her. There are times in every boy's life when he realizes he still needs his mom. Even though we weren't as tight as we were when I was a little boy, I missed her nurturing and needed her unconditional love. I was spiraling out of control. She never said anything to me, but she knew that when I asked to come home, what I was really doing was reaching out for her help.

I had become so introverted. Mom and I used to talk about everything when I was younger, but now I had completely withdrawn from her. From the time I started playing guitar, I used to sit and talk to her about my dreams of leaving Bakersfield and moving to Hollywood to become a rock star. She was always encouraging, even when I was too young and naive to really understand what achieving all of my dreams meant in terms of commitment and dedication to my craft to really make it. Mom never made me feel judged for my excessive partying. Her biggest concern was always for my safety. As long as I wasn't driving she didn't care if I came home wasted. It didn't matter what time I stumbled through the door. She was always in the kitchen waiting for me, hoping I would open up to her while she made me something to eat.

I didn't know it at the time, but Dad could see that I was headed for real trouble so he called Mom to say that I needed to live with her for a while. Once I moved back home, I slowly started to open up again like I did when I was younger. Whenever Mom tried to talk about what was going on with me, I'd tell her everything was fine. I thought I was pretty convincing, too. Even so, she knew better.

I really don't know why I retreated the way I did. Maybe it was my hurt from the divorce or maybe it was from all of my drug and alcohol abuse. I wasn't angry with anyone in particular—I was just angry. Whatever the reasons, I was home where I felt safe and secure. Mom's unconditional love and support gave me the freedom to pursue my dream, which was the only thing I truly cared about.

CHAPTER 2

MAKE ME BAD

My dream to become a rock star was always vivid and clear. I always knew I would some-day make it big. I could literally see myself in a band, playing big arenas to sold-out crowds around the world. The words *can't* or *won't* never entered my mind. I was going to succeed no matter what. I never put that goal second to any others, which is what I think drove me to practice—as hard and as often as possible. I made it a priority to never miss band practice. When someone else didn't approach the band with the same commitment and dedication, it became a real problem.

In fact, toward the end of high school, Pierced fell apart because our lead singer just couldn't commit. He was more into his girlfriend than he was the band, so it was challenging to get him to show up. When he left, we disassembled Pierced and I joined Ragtime, a group started by my friend Richard Moral. He was looking for a bass player, so I started to fill in. Head played with us, too, but the overall chemistry never felt

Early days of L.A.P.D. at our rehearsal spot. My first bass and speaker cabinet set-up—two 15s and four 10s.

quite right. We ended up wanting to go in different directions so that's what we did.

Richard and I were both friends with Munky, who, like Head, was also a fantastic guitarist. Even though he didn't play with Pierced, I thought it might be cool to start a band with him. We still needed a lead singer. That's when we met Pete Capra. Even though he had never sung in a band before, Pete had an awesome ear for music. He turned us on to bands like the Red Hot Chili Peppers and Faith No More. Munky and I loved what we heard. Those bands sounded like the direction we were trying for ourselves so we started writing music that fit that funk rock sound.

Together, we started another band and called ourselves

David Silveria on the drums in L.A.P.D.'s rehearsal space.

L.A.P.D., which originally stood for "Love and Peace, Dude." Before we would be complete, though, we still needed to find a drummer. We placed an ad in the local paper that read:

Funk, thrash, metal groove band looking for drummer.

David Silveria answered the ad by leaving a message on my answering machine. He said he was looking for a band and that he could play funk, thrash, metal groove. He wasn't even old enough to drive yet, so we auditioned David in his parents' garage. We liked what we heard—a lot. We started writing music together that same day.

The first song I wrote for L.A.P.D. stemmed from a bass line I had had in my head for months. I had the guitar line and drumbeat down too. Richard put the lyrics to it and called the song "Jesus." It was a really heavy song. I had no connection to it in terms of its religious meaning—I just liked the sound.

Jesus, take me in your arms.
Jesus where do I belong.
Matter of fact, life is kind of boring.
Drugs and crime are my glory.

We knew it was a good song so we started working on a couple more until we had four songs pulled together to make a demo we could send to record companies: "James Brown," "Stinging Like a Bee," "Jesus," and "Don't Label Me."

It was obvious that we had to leave Bakersfield if we were going to make it to the big time. Richard, David, and I wanted to move down to Hollywood so we could be closer to the rock movement that was so prominent in L.A. We knew that Hollywood was where all of the best musicians hung out and where the metal music scene was at, especially if we were going to get signed to a major record label. Munky didn't want to go because he had a girlfriend in Bakersfield. David was still in high school, so leaving meant he'd have to drop out and he did. I can see how it was a big and somewhat scary move for some of the guys, but it was a risk I was willing to take to make my dream come true. I had no fear about leaving home. I told my mother the guys and me were moving to L.A. to become stars. She smiled a knowing smile, as if to say, "Of course you are." She meant it, too. Mom always told me I had something special. She said Dad was a great musician but that I was a born entertainer. I could hardly wait for what lurked around the next corner of my life. My dream was right in front of me and I had the guts to chase it.

Richard, David, and I drove my pickup from Bakersfield to Burbank, where we crashed at Richard's mom Donna's two-bedroom apartment. Donna was really great to let us all invade her tiny space. In fact, David was so young when we moved to Burbank that his mother asked Donna if she would formally take legal custody of him until he turned eighteen, which she did. Eventually, Munky came to L.A., too. Head began having problems with his girl so he called to say he was coming down to visit us and to check out the music scene. He thought he might start his own band, so not long after Munky arrived, Head showed up, too.

It didn't take a lot of convincing to get Head to stay for good. By the time he arrived, eight of us were living with Donna. There were mattresses all over the place. My room was literally a closet. I had a single bed stuffed inside this walk-in closet. All the other guys had their beds scattered around the living room with no privacy at all. I didn't mind the closet because I could actually close the door if I wanted to get away.

Shortly after we got settled in, we found a rehearsal space in the heart of Hollywood right off Western Avenue. (An interesting side note is that Korn's current studio is two blocks from where L.A.P.D. used to practice.) A lot of fledgling bands practiced in the same complex, including Gerk and Ruckus, who eventually became the Electric Love Hogs, the band that spawned Goldfinger's John Feldmann. There were always fifteen or more bands in the studio and most of the time, it was one big party.

We were still somewhat inspired by the work of the Red Hot Chili Peppers, but we wanted to strike our own sound. We saw the guys from the Chili Peppers around Hollywood from time to time but had never really met them. They rehearsed close to our space and I'd catch a glimpse every now and then. One afternoon Head and I were coming out of the studio and for some reason, I can't recall why, we got into an argument. It wasn't unusual back then because I could be a mean bastard—especially if I had been drinking. That's just the way I was when I partied. I never gave much thought to the words that uncontrollably flew out of my mouth. I cut people down, made nasty comments, and generally didn't care who I spoke to in that way.

I'm certain I said something to piss off Head that particular day. My mouth was always just running. What I do recall is standing on the street arguing with Head when he threw an unexpected kick at me. I grabbed his leg, catching it in midair, and started dragging him down the street. We ended up on the ground wrestling like two punks. I got Head back up on his feet and started dragging him around some more when I noticed Anthony Kiedis and Chad, the drummer from the Chili Peppers at the time, coming toward us. I still had Head's leg in my hands, still dragging him along as we passed

Anthony and Chad. Head and I started hysterically laughing because we suddenly realized that we must have looked like complete jerks.

I decided to say hello.

I said, "Hey, man. You're Anthony from the Chili Peppers. What's up?"

He looked at me kind of weird because I was, of course, still holding Head's leg.

"Our band practices here. You guys have really been a big influence on us. Would you come up and hear our songs?" I was really hoping he wouldn't turn me down.

Somehow, I was able to convince him to come to the studio later that night. We played so hard, jumping up and down, trying to give a great performance. Our singer went nuts, pulling his PA speakers off the wall and smashing them to the ground. Stuff went flying everywhere. Anthony and Chad were standing there sort of dumbfounded—and not in a good way. We must have been so sloppy because we were obviously drunk and out of control. We didn't know any better. We just thought we were doing what we were supposed to do.

I don't know that Anthony will remember that night, but I'll never forget it. Hopefully, he was as wasted as we were and won't remember a thing!

Even though there were five of us in the band, we had a hard time coming up with the rent every month. None of us had real jobs, so there was no real money coming in—at all. We were living off the limited money we had saved before moving to L.A. or finding innovative ways to make a few bucks.

One of the most memorable jobs we had was when all of us started working for a time-share company. We didn't have to sell a thing. All we had to do was get people to sign up for a free trip to Hawaii. The company had us set up in

Me and L.A.P.D.

front of grocery stores or at various trade shows at the convention center to attract potential customers. The spiel was the same. All someone had to do to get the free trip was sit through a ninety-minute presentation on the joys of time-share ownership.

The trips sounded better than they really were.

Of course, there's always a catch to everything that sounds too good to be true. Knowing that made it easier for us to come up with creative ways to scam the company we were working for. Instead of showing up to wherever we were supposed to be, we sat at home, filled out the forms using people's names we retrieved from the local phone books and turned in those sheets as potential leads. We really didn't *want* to work and definitely didn't want to be part of some scheme that conned people into "free" trips.

We wanted to be rock stars, not two-bit huckster salesmen.

Eventually, the company caught on to our scamming the scammers. They called us all into their office and accused us of filling out the forms with fake names. When we denied their claim, our boss got on the phone and called a few random numbers from our lists. Sure enough, the person who answered said they hadn't signed anything with regard to time shares. We were busted. Needless to say, they fired us on the spot.

Faking the leads seemed like a good idea at the time, but it didn't take us long to realize that without that job, we'd all be flat broke . . . again. We weren't making that much money with the time-share company, anyway—maybe a hundred dollars a week each—but collectively, it added up to be enough to sustain us and allow us to rent our rehearsal space and purchase just enough beer to get by.

Once we were officially unemployed, Munky and I began to panhandle on the streets of Hollywood to make a little money. We'd pull my pickup truck into a gas station and tell people we ran out of gas and ask if they could spare a couple of bucks to help us out. We'd sit there and bum money until we could buy just enough gas to get to the studio and some beer for the night. Since money was so tight, we used to drink Ballentine beer—the cheapest we could find. It's all we could afford, especially because we were drinking every day. And then, one day someone found an even cheaper beer called St. Ides, which was a malt liquor all the rappers liked to drink. It was a buck thirty-nine for a forty-ounce can. I was starting to get way into rap at this point, so even though that brew was nasty, I really didn't mind drinking their beer of choice. I do remember drinking a couple of those forties and throwing up or worse, dry heaving because it tasted so gross. Everyone used to laugh at me because I was always getting sick from drinking St. Ides.

This is when my problems with dry heaving started. My nerves were really shot from partying so much, living a fast life, and not being able to afford our rent. I didn't know it at the time, but my lifelong battle with anxiety definitely worsened when I moved to Burbank. I was living with eight guys in a small apartment, struggling to make ends meet, and chasing the dream. I had a good disposition on the outside, but inside, I was a mess. I was living in a walk-in closet, bumming money on the streets, and slowly realizing I was becoming an alcoholic.

Like most addicts, I self-medicated, using alcohol as a way to reduce my anxiety. I figured I could muscle down the uneasy feelings by forcing a forty or two down my throat. Once I got a little buzz, those jittery feelings went away. By the time I was completely drunk, I didn't care about anything. This cycle became an ongoing battle for me.

And even though I thought I had everything under control, things progressed and continued to get worse. I began shaking the moment I woke up in the morning. I couldn't control my breathing or my feelings of panic. I felt too bad to start drinking first thing in the morning. Most people who excessively party often have bouts of anxiety, though they might not realize what is actually bringing it on. When I was suffering from the night before, I'd do anything necessary to feel better. I used to hear people I partied with talk about certain drugs and how they helped with bad hangovers, so I started taking Xanax to calm myself down. Once the Xanax kicked in, I felt good enough to start drinking again. So this was the beginning of my vicious cycle of taking depressants with booze—a horrible combination, to be sure, but it became my definition of comfortable and familiar.

To make matters worse, somewhere in the midst of all of this I decided to get married to Sidney, a girl I barely knew. Sidney had long straight blond hair, blue eyes, a typical California beach girl. We first met at a party in Bakersfield when I was around nineteen. She spent more time in Los Angeles as we started to date. We got married a couple of years later when I was around twenty-one. I always felt that I got pressured into the wedding. Sidney was always asking me when I was going to "pop the question." I didn't want to get married but after hearing that question every day for months, I thought it was what she wanted me to do, so I agreed. I didn't really care one way or the other. While we were dating, I saw a poster on a light pole around Hollywood that said I could get a divorce for $175. I thought, "If I had to, I could scrounge up enough money to get out," so I went ahead and married her. To be honest, I was never in love with her but she was always good company.

Sidney and I moved into a small apartment in Huntington Beach. The rent was an astounding six hundred dollars a month, which was a lot of money to me back then since I was hardly making any. I had started selling weed as a way to make ends meet. Someone told me I could drive to Santa Ana to buy my stash from dealers who worked Flower Street. I was kind of nervous at first. I was buying an ounce of weed once a week. The dealer would bring the Baggie out onto the street, which made me even more skittish, because I was making my buys in broad daylight. I carried a small hand scale with me so I could weigh the bag before I paid for it. Inevitably, it was always a half ounce short. This went on every single week for about a year.

I was getting tired of the routine when I ran into an old friend from home who had become one of the biggest drug dealers back in Bakersfield. Carlos was a Mexican guy who wore his hair in a mullet. He was a real Rico Suave type. He told me he'd front me the weed so I no longer had to make the drive to Santa Ana. It sounded too good to be true, but I knew this guy and I wouldn't have to lay out any cash so I took him up on his offer. He gave me three pounds of weed to get rid of the first time around. It took me less than a week to move that entire inventory. Before I knew it, Carlos was stashing large garbage bags full of smoke inside my apartment and I was selling the stuff like crazy. It was overwhelming but I didn't care because it was free. Also, since I didn't smoke pot at the time, everything I had was pure profit. I never dipped into the stash.

Average pot is usually very dry. It's often called brick weed, which is primarily what I sold. To make even more money, I added a little extra weight by soaking the weed with water so it felt heavier than it was. I'd lay out all my weed, spray it down with a water bottle, bag it up, and sell it for more than it was worth. I could make an ounce of weed weigh out to be an ounce and a half just by moistening it up.

I started selling to everyone in Huntington Beach—even trading pot to pay for part of my rent with my landlord. He couldn't trade the entire rent because he didn't want his wife to know he was smoking weed, so we did a half cash–half weed deal every month. Other random people would come by my place, some daily, to buy from me. One surfer dude with killer dreads came by every single morning at 6:00 A.M. to buy an ounce off me. He once showed up with no money but left me his surfboard and wet suit as collateral. I fronted him the ounce and never saw him again. I'd have to listen to these stoners go on and on about something absurd before we could complete our transaction.

"Yo, dude. Have you ever looked at a twenty-dollar bill high on weed?" They'd talk about how awesome their twenty looked while high. It was ridiculous.

No one could walk through my door, buy their stuff, and leave without giving my some idiotic insight or crazy stoner story. I felt like that dude in the movie *Half Baked*. Dealing with those people sucked.

Eventually, I started getting nervous about the traffic in and out of my place so I started delivering to customers. At the time, I was driving an old 1967 Mercedes-Benz, which stood out in some of the neighborhoods I was going to, so I rode my bicycle to avoid any unwanted extra attention.

Business was really good. And even though I was uptight most of the time for fear of being busted, it didn't stop me from selling. And then, one week, Carlos didn't show up with my delivery. I didn't know what happened, but I knew something was up. I was getting really nervous because he was my sole source for weed and my income depended on him. Another week went by before someone said they read about Carlos in the Bakersfield newspaper. Apparently, Carlos went to Bakersfield to pick up his stash as usual. When he walked up to the guys he was buying from, they held a gun to his face and shot him. They put him in the trunk of their car, drove him to L.A., and dumped his body in a ditch. The police found him a few days later with his face completely blown off.

Needless to say, I was scared—frightened enough to get out of the business altogether. I never planned to sell drugs. It sort of fell into my lap. And it was so easy and convenient; plus, I was making fistfuls of cash. But when Carlos was killed, I knew that wasn't going to be my fate. His death saved my life. The only other thing I knew how to do was clean carpets, so I shifted gears.

My marriage to Sidney was a terribly violent relationship right from the start. I was verbally and physically abusive to her, usually when I was drunk or high. Although I never actually hit her, I often grabbed her, threw her around, dragged her across the floor, and treated her like dirt. Whenever I came home late, she always accused me of being out with other women. Women have a sixth sense about their men. She was right because I was never faithful to her. I didn't even try to hide it.

One night I came home especially late. I was holding my bass in one hand and a beer in the other.

"Where have you been?" she asked.

"Can't you tell?" I thought holding my bass made it clear. "I was at band practice." Of course, I was lying.

"I don't believe you. It's three o'clock in the morning." It was kind of late to be coming home from practice but I didn't like being accused of something, either—even if her instincts were right.

I was enraged by Sidney's accusation so I threw my bass at her. It hit her so hard, it knocked her to the floor. When she got up, she ran to the kitchen, grabbed a butcher knife, and came toward me like a crazed animal.

I wasn't scared. In fact, I was kind of amused by her reaction. "What are you going to do, stab me? Go ahead." I was practically taunting her.

Sidney was hysterically crying as she lunged forward wildly swinging at me. She cut open my shirt and made four shallow gashes in my chest. Now I was pissed. I totally flipped out. Instead of physically lashing back at her, I just shut down.

"I never want to see you again!" I turned and walked out the front door. I went to the L.A.P.D. band house where I knew there was a party going on. I wanted to get drunker than I already was so I could forget about what had happened. It was clear that our marriage was in trouble.

Not long after that fight, Sidney called me one day to ask if I had been cheating on her. She promised she wasn't going to leave me if I told her the truth, so I confessed everything. I had been with many women throughout our marriage, though none of them were more than a one-night stand. It was more than she could stand to hear. She ended the call by saying she was leaving, that the marriage was over.

At the time, I felt sad about the breakup, but I was a horrible husband. I didn't know you had to have morals to be married. I wanted the cake, the icing, the lit candles, everything without having to sacrifice in other areas of my life. Whenever you sit down to eat a whole cake, you always pay the price. I guess I deserved her leaving. My marriage ended the same time as my drug dealing. It was a crazy couple of years.

In the meantime, Richard and I were hustling to book the band some gigs. We'd get on the phone and just start calling around to all of the hot Hollywood clubs. L.A.P.D. booked a couple of dates around town, but most of the early shows were pay-to-play shows at clubs like the world-famous Whisky, Coconut Teazer, the Roxy, Gazzari's (which is now the Key Club) on the Sunset Strip.

"Pay to play" meant we had to buy all of the tickets in advance and sell them before the night of the show. I can't remember how much we had to pay for those tickets but I can tell you that at the time, it was a lot for us to be shelling out. We always came up with ways to sell those tickets, though, whether it was standing outside the venue for days and nights before the show or bumming money from friends to come see us play.

We made no money playing those shows. It was a lose or break-even scenario at best. You wouldn't have known it by the way I acted at the time but once again, I was finally flat-out broke. I was surviving on Top Ramen and cheap beer. It got so bad that I started selling my clothes to make ends meet. I tried to make a game out of my situation, convincing myself that I would someday look back on those days and know that I most certainly paid my dues. It was almost funny to me be-

L.A.P.D. rehearsing.

cause I knew I was going to make it and that these hard times would be left behind once we hit the big time.

After one particular show at Coconut Teazer, this guy named Arthur came to talk to us. He said he was trying to manage bands and wanted to handle L.A.P.D. At the time, we were young and believed everything we heard. When Arthur said he could get us a record deal, we thought, "cool" and signed with him. He seemed like such a good guy and really knew what was up. I trusted him from the day we met. Even though we didn't really need a manager, it was cool to say we had one, and it seemed like the logical next step if we were going to hit it big. Arthur ended up being more of a good friend than a true manager. We used to go to his house on Sundays to have band meetings and eat his homemade spaghetti. We'd all pile in Richard's Isuzu pickup truck (by this time, each of us had sold ours for the dough) to make the trip.

One day on our way to see Arthur, a cop pulled behind us, and I just knew he was going to pull us over because there were so many long-haired, crazy-looking dudes riding in the back of the pickup truck. At the time, there was a warrant out on Munky for a jaywalking ticket he never paid, so I said to him, "Give the cop a fake name or you'll go to jail." I had this feeling the cop was going to bust him. Something in my gut told me this wasn't going to end well. But Munky shrugged it off. He didn't even respond to me.

For whatever reason, Munky was wearing a pair of my shoes that day. I told him he'd have to take them off if he wasn't going to give the cop a different name because I didn't want him wearing my shoes to jail. I was joking around at first, but as the cop checked each of us for warrants one by one, I knew that Munky was going to be arrested. Sure enough, when they ran his name, his warrant came up.

"Take my shoes off," I told him. "I'm serious. I don't want you wearing my shoes to jail."

He did just seconds before the cop handcuffed him and hauled him off—completely barefoot. If that happened today, I'd give Munky the shirt off my back and the shoes off my feet. It was so childish and dumb, and I regret making him go through that, but at the time I was just being a jerk. Sometimes you do stuff when you're younger for no good reason. That doesn't make it right and it isn't being a good friend. I know that today, and even though he brings it up from time to time, I really hope that deep down, Munky knows it was just an immature prank.

Things were getting worse for all of us. Since we didn't have any money, we had to stop paying rent on our rehearsal space. We got very good at dodging our landlord, and we were a solid three or four months behind when he finally caught up with us. Because Richard was the lead singer, we all thought he should do the talking. He tried to explain that we simply didn't have the money, but our landlord didn't want to hear our lame excuses. He gave us an ultimatum. Either we paid the rent in full or we had to get out.

We are not the type of guys who took ultimatums very well. Their conversation escalated a little until they were almost arguing.

Richard finally stood up, got right in the guy's face, and said, "I guess we're going to have to fight it out."

We were all stunned because Richard wasn't an especially violent guy nor was he a big dude. Thankfully, nothing physical happened, but the landlord did end up padlocking and chaining the door shut with all of our equipment locked inside. When we discovered what he had done, we left without saying a word only to return later that night. There was no way we were leaving all of our equipment behind. We busted down the door to get our stuff.

We found another studio the next day, but it was in Santa Monica, which was a lot farther away from Burbank than Hollywood. Richard was the only one with a vehicle, so we'd all pile into the back cab of his pickup to make the forty-five-minute drive. It was kind of funny to see eight grown men squished in the back of a truck like that, but we did whatever it took to get to rehearsal.

A buzz starting building about L.A.P.D. We continued playing shows all around the L.A. area, but there seemed to be a curse of sorts that plagued us wherever we'd go. Something always went wrong. I usually broke four or five bass strings per show, which wasn't all that unexpected, but losing power or having our mics cut out was never anticipated. No matter what happened, though, we always dealt with the situation—as they say, the show must go on.

Luckily, audiences loved us. Richard was a crazy dude onstage. One night he decided to wear nylons on his head. He filled the legs with eggs. He would dangle them back and forth so they would crack open all over the crowd. He liked to pour beer on the stage and pretend to swim in the puddles. He even came out dressed like Ronald McDonald for one show, wearing a red curly wig, a McDonald's visor, and a full on uniform. He actually got a job at McDonald's just to get the uniform, then quit soon after he started. It was hilarious to see him do a whole show dressed like that.

I started wearing pipe cleaners in my hair. I had dreads back then, so when I wrapped the bright green, red, yellow, and blue pipe cleaners in, you could really see them in the stage lights. Sometimes I'd wear swim fins on stage and over-sized sunglasses (like the ones a clown would wear). I once took the springs out of my mattress and taped them to the bottom of my shoes so I could bounce around stage. It didn't really work, but I thought it looked kind of cool. Even though we were kind of goofy, our music was very heavy. We had a good sound that was probably ahead of its time. I think L.A.P.D.'s music holds up to this day.

In 1990, Arthur introduced us to an executive from Triple X Records, a small independent record company, who saw us play one particular show at the Whisky. Triple X was (or is) the label for bands such as Bo Diddley, the Vandals, Jane's Addiction, Social Distortion, Dr. Dre, Weeto, DTTX, Mr. Shadow, Lil Blacky, and Brown Boy, just to name a few. The executive loved our sound and offered us a contract to record for his label. We thought we were going to be the biggest rock band in the world. We knew a lot of the bands on their label. We thought we had struck gold and were lured by the promise of going into the studio to record our first album. In our naive way, we believed getting signed to a record company was the hardest part of success. Man, were we mistaken.

It was a pitiful contract, but at the time it was everything we had ever dreamed of. I thought it was our big break—my dream come true. We didn't know enough to realize there wasn't enough money in the contract for all of us to survive, let alone record. There was no budget for anything. I think the record company gave us five grand to cut the first album. I had absolutely nothing and now I was recording for no money. I didn't figure that into the equation when I dreamed of becoming a rich and famous rock star.

Once again, I didn't really care because all I wanted to do was record an album. I was willing to do whatever it took to make it. Since I was forced to sell my Benz, I had to hitch-hike to the studio with my bass in hand. Incredibly, I made it there every day. I've always been a pretty determined guy who never let anything stand in my way. No money? No problem! Everything always had a way of working out.

While recording, the guys and I pooled our money to share Del Taco so we could eat while working at the studio. It was kind of funny watching us carefully split up the burritos into five even pieces. They were rough times for sure, but I wouldn't have changed a thing. I learned to live that crazy, poor, struggling life with the same cool and happy intoxicated spirit I always had. Though I still battled my anxiety, I never cared all that much about how I lived. I still don't. If I lost everything today, I know I could still make do. Not caring gives me a certain security in knowing that I would survive no matter what.

When we finished the album, we realized we'd put in so much work and had very little to show for our efforts. Yes, we had an album, but we still had no money. None of us had enough money to be out on our own. It was frustrating and confusing. And, to make matters worse, Donna finally got sick of us living in her apartment. Thankfully, Munky's dad lived in Long Beach, so we all moved in with him for a while.

We thought that a record deal meant touring and arenas. That was a misguided notion, since the record company had no budget for that. Triple X wouldn't get behind us, and we didn't have the knowledge or experience to force them.

Needless to say, we learned a lot from that first deal. Eventually, all of us except for Richard wanted out. In the end, we were a band that spent most of our time practicing the same songs over and over again and getting stone-cold drunk. L.A.P.D. was really going nowhere. Our deal sucked, our album wasn't being distributed properly, and we were still dirt poor. We did a couple of good songs together, but I knew there had to be something more.

I didn't want to stay with Triple X. We all thought we could do better someplace else. They hadn't set the bar very high so it's not like we were walking away from anything. Richard disagreed. He was adamant about staying with Triple X. The rest of us were done. We thought our easiest way out would be to dump all of our songs, quit, and start all over. We agreed that we wouldn't even keep the name of the band. We eventually told Arthur the band was breaking up and that all of us were going separate ways. He was cool about it.

So, Munky, David, and I had to start all over again. Richard refused to come with us, so we needed a lead singer, and we put out the word to everyone we knew. In the meantime, we headed back to the studio and started writing music morning, noon, and night. We just wanted to keep making music— even if we were in between record companies.

The music we created was really good, but we were still short a singer. We worked with Corey, a guy we knew from around town for a while who had a pretty cool voice. His image was so perfect for our band, like the ideal rock star, with the whitest skin I ever saw, long straight red hair that was down to the middle of his back, and a matching goatee. He dyed both this extreme fire engine red color—a color that wasn't natural looking at all but was really cool. He always wore long cutoff shorts and had lots of tattoos and these very intense piercing baby blue eyes.

We decided to cut a demo with him but he was impossible to get along with, a little quirky and weird. He always made his girlfriend sit in the car while the band rehearsed. We told Corey it was fine to have her come in while we practiced, but he'd make her sit in the car for hours on end until we were done. Corey would ask Munky to take his hair out of his ponytail because it was "messing with his vibe." He'd go from being completely mellow and cool to suddenly ranting and screaming. If we were playing the song wrong, he would get completely pissed off. It was like we had to walk on eggshells all the time. It was so different from the vibe we shared in L.A.P.D., where we all wanted to laugh and have a good time. Even though it wasn't working out with Corey, we couldn't fire the guy because we needed a singer.

Head was hanging out with us a lot at the time. He always sat on the sidelines and listened to us play. I always knew he was one of the best musicians in the world and didn't understand why he wasn't just playing with us. I finally told Munky I wanted to ask Head to join the band. I thought it would be great to have two guitars going. It would make our music sound bigger, fuller, and more powerful. Head was at the point where he was about to pack it in and go back to Bakersfield to go work at his dad's Chevron station. I couldn't see wasting his talent that way, so just before he was supposed to leave, I asked him to join the band. He agreed to stay. We formed a new band called Creep. Together, we created the sound that would be the prelude to the sound of Korn today.

Not long after Head joined the band, we ran into Ross Robinson, an old friend and extremely talented musician and producer. We ended up doing our first Creep demo with him. We recorded nine songs, which was challenging because our singer was still being incredibly difficult. It had become obvious that he couldn't stay. As had become customary, we took a vote. None of us wanted to work with him. It was unanimous—he had to go.

I had the dubious honor of having to call Corey to tell him that we no longer wanted him in the band. He and I were pretty good friends so it wasn't a call I was looking forward to making. When I broke the news to Corey, for whatever reason, he didn't believe me at first. He was actually laughing as I tried to convince him that the band was really letting him go. When I was unable to persuade him that I was being sincere, he called Munky and David to ask if I was telling the truth. But, when he called, they refused to answer their phones. They didn't want to talk to him. When he was unable to get confirmation from the other guys, Corey called me back. He was still sure that I was playing a prank on him. But this was no joke. As hard as it was, I had to stand firm. He called me for a solid week until it finally sunk in that it was over. It was like having a girlfriend who was in denial after a bad breakup. Once he realized he was really out, I never heard from him again.

I felt bad about having to do that to a friend. I still listen to the Creep demo from time to time and think it's really good. We were all so young. I am sure things would be different if we saw each other today. Maybe Corey and I will have the chance to mend fences. Who knows? Maybe we'll even record together again someday.

After I fired Corey, we were once again a band without a singer. We got really good at playing long instrumental music. It was real heavy but kind of funky, too. But, without a lead singer, the band couldn't book any gigs. That gave each of us the opportunity to break away and take some time off. I hung out in Hollywood because I didn't have enough money to do anything else. Munky and Head took off for Bakersfield to visit their families. One night, they went out to a local bar where they saw some band but were pretty unimpressed with what they heard. Just as they were leaving, they heard this powerful voice coming from the stage. They described it as the craziest, coolest Dutch voice they'd ever heard. They looked back at the dude on the stage and he was dressed like a drag queen. He was wearing a dress, makeup, the full look. The guys didn't care because his voice was mesmerizing. When they came back to L.A. to rehearse, they told me all about the singer they'd heard back in Bakersfield.

"What was his name?" I figured I probably knew him since I was well aware of all the great musicians in Bakersfield.

"We asked around. We were told his name is Jonathan Davis."

At the time, Jon was playing in a band called Sexart. Ryan, the guitarist, became the guitar player for Orgy, a band Korn later signed to our own label. The bass player from Sexart ended up in a band called Adema, where Jon's stepbrother Marky was the lead singer. There sure was a lot of talent that came out of Bakersfield in those days.

I told Munky and Head that my mom used to babysit Jonathan when he was a kid and that my dad played in a band with his dad.

"I can get ahold of him, no problem." I made the call the next day. When Jon and I started talking, we mostly kept the conversation about music. I told him I was really into a darker heavy sound. He said he loved that kind of music because you don't have to sing in key.

When I heard him say that, I remember thinking, *This is never going to work.* Later, of course, I realized that what he meant was that he could sing in a minor key, not that he wanted to sing out of tune. The guy can sing perfectly in key, but I initially mistook what he was saying.

Even though I had my doubts, Munky and Head were crazy about his voice so I asked Jon if he was interested in coming down to L.A. to meet with the band. He was reluctant at first, saying he didn't want to leave Sexart. Since I had a bit of background in telemarketing, I knew the guys would never forgive me if I didn't close the deal, so I laid it on as thick as I could. I told Jon we had a record company that was interested in us, a big-time producer, management, shows booked in Hollywood, and that we were on our way to touring all around the world. I really had to sell the whole deal, even offering to pay for him to come to Hollywood. I told Jon he didn't have to worry about a thing. If he didn't like what he heard, we'd get him a bus ticket home, no problem. Finally, and after a lot of selling on my part, he agreed.

A couple of days later, Head and I went to the Hollywood bus depot and waited for Jon. When he stepped off the bus, he had red, almost burgundy, dyed shoulder-length hair. He was wearing these big silver hoop earrings, lots of makeup, ripped jeans with holes all through them, and zebra spandex leggings underneath. His top looked a little like a woman's blouse with a big open back. I guess this was a look he developed for Sexart. Apparently, Jon often wore skirts or dresses onstage, like on the night Munky and Head saw him. I didn't know what to make of it.

I turned to Head and said, "This guy is not going to work out."

Creep was going for a totally different image and style. We were more into the baggy hip-hop street way of dressing. I had dreadlocks. There was absolutely nothing femme about us.

Head pleaded with me, "His voice is phenomenal. It's insane. You've got to hear it before you make up your mind."

I didn't care what his voice sounded like; I didn't think Jonathan would fit in. Even so, I could tell Head was being sincere so I owed it to him to hear the guy sing.

We took him to the studio where he tried out. We played all of our songs for him—once. He was completely silent. Later he told me he was so quiet because he was completely blown away by what he heard. At the time, though, I wasn't sure if he liked our stuff or not. He asked if he could try singing one of the songs. We started playing. The second we started, he began making up his own words because we didn't really have set lyrics yet. All we had was the music. He had a distortion pedal he hooked up through his microphone that he was screaming through. From beginning to end, he sang the song perfect. He didn't sound like anything I had ever heard. It was completely different from our last singer—and it was just what our band needed.

I thought, *Man, it's on. This is the guy.* And he knew it, too. Jon had the biggest smile on his face as he said, "This is my band. You're my guys."

We all knew something special happened in the studio that day. We couldn't have been more excited or motivated to start making music together. Jon loved the heavy sound we had but he didn't especially care for the funky grooves. It was a no-brainer to drop the funk. We wanted to make this band work. And he was right. We needed to pick a direction and stick with it, so we went the heavy route.

Even though things went really well, I still had to convince Jon to quit Sexart and move down to L.A. He was reluctant because he didn't want to leave his band or quit his day job as a coroner. He was the guy who literally picked up bodies off the streets. I couldn't believe some of the stuff he told me about the dead people he'd seen. He told me about the time he brought home a dead fetus they found in a jar. He kept it on a shelf to show to all of his friends. He also liked to talk about a bloody body bag he kept after recovering a body from a crime scene. Jon loved to tell everyone about how he could gut a human being in under a minute by cutting him open

An early Korn gig
at Club 5902 in
Huntington Beach,
California, 1993.

and somehow grabbing the tongue and pulling everything out like you would do to a fish. His stories never grossed me out. They're just a part of who the guy was. Despite the morbid nature of his job, it paid really good money so it was hard to convince him to play with us—a fledgling band making absolutely nothing. Somehow, incredibly, he saw the same potential I did and decided to make the move, anyway.

Jon moved into my place for a few weeks until he could line up his own place. He eventually moved into my good friend Jeff Creath's garage in Huntington Beach where he lived for free until he could get settled.

And though we hadn't picked a name yet, soon after Jonathan moved to L.A., what would become Korn was born in 1993.

NO PLACE TO HIDE

As the band was getting off the ground and as a way to conserve our limited cash, we all decided to move into a small house together in Huntington Beach, about an hour south of L.A. I slept on the couch because anyone who had his own bedroom had to pay more rent. Head made up a small curtained-off room in the front entryway and everyone else took the bedrooms. We started working on a bunch of new songs. It was time to find a new rehearsal space so we could work through the creative process and start making music. We ended up renting a studio from Jeff Creath, the same guy who had let Jon live in his garage, a place he called "Underground Chicken Sound." It was pretty close to the house, so it was a perfect setup.

On our first day of rehearsal, a bunch of guys we didn't know were hanging around the studio. Since no one knew what we were about in Huntington, to them we were just a bunch of strange, dreadlock-wearing, messy-looking musi-

Receiving our certified gold album plaque for Korn's first record after a show with producer Ross Robinson.

cians. When we started playing, making these weird feed-back sounds they'd never heard, it must have sounded like we didn't know what we were doing. I could tell they were kind of thinking we were a bunch of wannabes. But those sounds were actually part of the song. (It later became the opening to "Clown," one of the songs off our first album, *Korn*.)

When we finally kicked into our first song, everyone in the studio freaked out. Everyone loved what they heard, especially Jeff. To be straight up, it was the craziest groove. Everyone's jaw dropped because it was so different. We didn't think it was all that unusual, because we were just doing what we do. When Jon started singing, the small crowd that had gathered was tripping out. We went off and just did our thing—jumping, banging our heads, thrashing about, putting on a full show. An hour later, when we finally put down our guitars, we had made a bunch of new friends.

We needed a name for the band. We decided to take a walk down to the Huntington Beach pier to brainstorm. We tossed a bunch of names around and talked about bands like Primus, the Beatles, Faith No More, and several others we thought were cool, but figured their names probably didn't sound cool at first. We wanted a name like that. I don't know who said it, but someone suggested the name *Corn*. All of us thought it sounded stupid at first. Everyone hated it, especially Larry, who was our manager at the time. We told Larry we were going to use it anyway. He was adamant, saying that there was no way we should use the name Corn. He didn't think we'd ever land a record deal with such a dumb name. Someone jokingly told Larry we could always call the band *Larry* and put his face on the cover of our first album, but that didn't go over too well, either.

So the decision was made. We would call ourselves Corn.

As a way to make it stand out a little, someone suggested spelling it with a K instead of a C. Munky had the idea to make the "R" appear backward so it looked like a little kid drew it. We all thought that sounded great. And so, the era of Korn was born.

It was time to start spreading the word that Korn was in town. We wanted everyone from Huntington Beach to Hollywood asking, "What is Korn?" Jeff said he knew a guy who was a screen printer who could make T-shirts for us. Head drew up some designs using these funky cartoon characters of us for the shirts. We came up with a few different designs and started selling or giving the shirts away. We had bumper stickers made, too, and slapped them up all over Huntington Beach.

As a way to help pay our rent at the studio, we used to throw these wild parties where we charged ten dollars to get in and we'd play for a bunch of random people who would show up. We had the studio set up like a small nightclub. We kept the lights dimmed and blasted hip-hop music, especially Cypress Hill, before our set. When it came time for us to play, we'd shut all the music off and hit it.

Up to this point, we hadn't yet played our first professional gig as Korn. We were just trying to pay the rent and create great songs. We had started to build a pretty strong local following—enough to make us certain we could fill one of the clubs back up in Hollywood. We booked our first show at a local strip club in Anaheim. The crowd loved us.

With a little experience under our belt, we were ready to book a show at the Whisky. Like the shows we did as L.A.P.D., that first Hollywood gig was a pay-to-play deal. This time, we came up with an idea to charter a bus, put a keg on it, and bring the fans with us. We were making a name for ourselves locally, so it made sense to bring a captive audience to Holly-

wood instead of trying to captivate the Hollywood audience.
Plus, we wanted the venue full of Korn lovers. We charged
thirty dollars to get on the bus. In exchange for that, we pro-
vided a ride to Hollywood, a couple of beers, a great show,
and a ride back to Huntington Beach. It was easy to get thirty
or more people together so we always covered our costs. It
didn't take long for us to have enough people to charter two
buses.

With sixty people from Huntington and the spreading
word of mouth, the buzz was beginning to grow. We played
a few more shows at the Whisky and the Roxy. People were
flipping out. We knew we had something different, and it felt
really good. Up until Jon joined the band, there was always
something missing. We could never really put our finger on
it, but we all knew the chemistry wasn't quite right until Jon
came onboard. When you get four or five guys together who
gel, there's a force that takes over. We knew we had it, and
we were definitely doing something that no one else could do.
Some record companies were beginning to take notice, too.

Executives from Warner Brothers and Epic Records came
to talk about signing us. They kept telling us we were going to
be the next Guns N' Roses or Stone Temple Pilots. We didn't
want to be like those bands. When we told those label guys it
wasn't what we wanted, they seemed confused. We would sit
around for hours and talk about why no one seemed to know
what to do with Korn. We had something so different—we
didn't want to get thrown into the grunge metal genre. We
wanted to create our own category of music that set the bar
for other bands to be like.

Finally we met Paul Pontius, an executive from Immortal
Records. We knew they recorded Cypress Hill, a band we
loved; House of Pain; and Funkdoobiest, another band we

were really into. Paul came to see a couple of our shows, but never told us he was there until we sat down to talk with him.

He said, "I know what you guys are doing. I get what you're all about, and I think it's really cool." He talked about our hip-hop undertones combined with the metal sound. He recognized our street wear as much as he identified our sound. He explained everything about Korn better than we ever could. This was the guy we'd been waiting for. It wasn't the amount of money or the deal he was offering. It was his innate understanding of Korn that was our primary reason for signing with Immortal. He knew exactly what to do with us. He immediately talked about getting us out on tour with Biohazard and House of Pain. At the time, that was like an insane dream come true. Everything that came out of Paul's mouth was exactly what we wanted to hear. We signed with Immortal and set out to record our first album as Korn.

We called our old friend Ross Robinson and asked if he would produce the album. He told us he had this great studio setup, called the Indigo Ranch, in the hills of Malibu. He said it was secluded and thought it would be a perfect spot for us to record the album. It was in the middle of nowhere, with a single, narrow one-way gravel road that led in and out. If you were wasted, which we usually were, you were staying put. It was way too dangerous to try and navigate those roads under the influence. So, in a way, it was a perfect setup for us. There was a large cabin on the property so we could sleep up there; since we wouldn't have to make the commute from Huntington, it became even more desirable.

Being at the Indigo Ranch was insane. We were trapped in the mountains doing the two things I love most—recording and partying. It was a thirty-minute drive to the nearest town so once we got there, we pretty much stayed put.

Ross was really into health and fitness so he'd get all of us to go hiking with him in the mornings. We'd carefully navigate down a steep trail that led to a river at the bottom of the canyon that surrounded the ranch. It wasn't an easy hike to begin with, but we were all doing it either wasted or completely hungover. Regardless, we always showed up and did it anyway. One day we got caught in a field of foot-high shrubs. We had to crawl on our hands and knees for forty-five minutes until we finally hit a clearing. When I came out of the woods, I saw chicken wire, live as well as dead chickens, and crosses everywhere. Clearly we were someplace we didn't want to be. It freaked me out so much that I sprinted all the way back to the ranch as fast as I could. I think some weird stuff was going on up in those hills. Thankfully, I never went back to that same spot so I never knew for sure, but it sure looked strange to me.

Living on the mountain for three months made me begin to feel like a real hillbilly. All five of us slept in a small single room next to the studio that was built on stilts. There was no air-conditioning, flies everywhere that landed on my face while I was trying to sleep, with the nearest bathroom being in the studio, which was close but felt very far away when you really had to go. It was rustic and not really my thing, although it did inspire us to create what became the classic Korn sound.

We were all so happy to be living the fairy-tale dream. I couldn't believe we were actually getting paid to do what we loved. After so many years of struggling and starving, all of my dreams were beginning to come true. It was all so new and exciting.

Making our first album brought out the best in all of us. There were a lot of laughs and a few practical jokes along the way. One afternoon while doing an interview for a television show, the five of us got into our version of a food fight. We were all eating sunflower seeds during the interview when suddenly Head spit a sunflower seed at Jon that stuck to his cheek. Jon was a good sport about it, laughing it off like it was no big deal. A few minutes later, he put a couple sunflower seeds in his mouth and spit them back at Head. I jumped in and hit Jon with a handful of seeds from my mouth that stuck to the other side of his face. Before we knew it, we were all spitting seeds at one another and pouring our beers over one another's heads, laughing and having a great time. The cameraman's and the reporter's jaws were on the ground in total disbelief at our obnoxious behavior. We didn't care. This is who we were.

Even with all of the fun and frivolity, life inside the studio was pretty intense. We recorded most of our first album raw, using vintage sounds. We used old tube amps, older-style guitars, and a particular pedal we found, called a Big Muff, which we combined with a Marshall amp, which gave Korn the distinctive sound we have today.

Because of the heavy nature of our music, we preferred to keep the lights dimmed and always had lots of candles burning to create the kind of peaceful atmosphere that helped us bring out the type of sound we were creating. The soft lighting inspires us to get really deep.

When we'd arrive at the control room, one of the techs had all of our instruments already amped up and ready to go. We'd put our headphones on and get ready to record. Ross always stood in the room with us while we recorded instead of remaining behind the glass partition in the studio. He'd get so excited about what he was hearing that he'd scream at the top of his lungs. If you listen closely to the album, you can actually faintly hear him screaming in the background.

We recorded that album all together, take by take. Sometimes bands lay down each instrument on separate tracks and then mix the song. Not us, at least not back then. We like jamming together. Once we started playing, there was a complete sense of concentration among all of us. It was truly the *only* time we were all focused. I think that synchronicity comes through in our sound. Once we were ready to record, we'd go into the studio where Head and Munky would come up with a heavy guitar riff while I'd lay a bass line over it, and before we knew it, a song would start. We could bust out a song in a day. It was easy because we were just playing the music we liked to listen to. Most of the scratch tracks from that first album ended up being original takes because there was such a connected vibe. When we were done with a perfect take, we all knew that would be the one to make the album. We'd throw off our headphones, go into the control room, and listen to the song on the two huge loudspeakers the size of a Scion that hung on the front wall of the studio. We'd listen back to the takes and get the chills and teary at what we heard. I don't think any Korn song ever made it onto the final album unless the band looked over at me and saw me crying.

Music moves me. It's the one thing that really gets me emotional and can make me cry. It's not so much the lyrics as it is the music itself. When I listen to music I hear a vibe. When there's an undeniable chemistry in the creation of music, it gets me to the core. I've always felt that way, and working with the other guys in the band gives me that sensation every single time we go into the studio to record.

Recording the song "Shoots and Ladders" was especially memorable because that was when Jon introduced bagpipes to our sound. He took his bagpipes to the top of the mountain that overlooked the whole canyon so we would record him playing with the natural acoustics. We ran lead cords all the way up the mountain to mic him so we could record the sound live in the studio. I went up to hang out with Jon when he first started to play. It was incredible to pick up the natural sounds of the canyon while he blew the pipes, truly breathtaking.

I eventually made my way back to the studio so I could hear what it sounded like in that environment. When I heard it for the first time, I think we all knew Jon's bagpipes would become a part of Korn's trademark.

As we progressed with our music, we'd invite all of our friends up to the ranch to listen to what we recorded and to hang out. We made bonfires and always had barbecues, where there was usually fresh corn on the grill. (No, that's not a joke!) We'd sometimes get sixty or more random friends together that ranged from the guys from Orgy to various girlfriends we all had. There were always kegs and lots of drugs, but everyone was pretty private about their personal use. I often wondered why everyone would disappear into the bathroom. At the time, the guys were into speed, but I wasn't into that then. I was usually getting drunk and taking downers. We were all drinking a lot. If you didn't drink a case of beer all by yourself, you were considered a sissy or a wimp. This went on every day, seven days a week for three months while we recorded.

Even though we were making an album, contractually, I was only making around six hundred dollars a month. Fame and fortune hadn't quite landed, but we all knew it was coming. So, to celebrate our success, even though we couldn't afford them, we all bought new cars. I got a Mercedes 190E, the cheapest car they made, but man, it was still a brand-new

I was so proud of my new Mercedes.

Mercedes so I didn't care. I was stoked. I put some fancy rims on the car and thought I was the man.

Finally, I thought. I could actually breathe a sigh of relief. For the first time in years, I wasn't struggling.

We had a slew of songs written already, but we wanted to create a few new songs, too. We actually cut out the top of a pizza box and pretended it was our first gold record. It served as our inspiration to do the best work we could. We were all extremely dedicated to making Korn a success. As hard as we partied the night before, we'd wake up the next morning, have just enough time to take a shower, and then head into the studio to make music. We'd take breaks here and there, but our focus was on work.

It was around the same time that we decided to start meeting with new potential managers. Larry ended up getting an offer to go to work for A&M Records. He wasn't making any money working for Korn, so he took the offer. Even though he would later tell us he made a huge mistake, he had to make the move at the time because it was too good to pass up.

Once again, it seemed like everyone we met with didn't get what we were all about. That is, until we met with Jeff Kwatinetz and Peter Katsis. Peter showed up at our meeting wearing all black and a bulky silver necklace that looked like an ankh, an Egyptian cross. Pete's a huge guy who stands around six foot nine inches, so he was a little intimidating. Jeff is equally tall but looked more like a lawyer. He was superskinny and kind of *GQ* looking. Meeting them reminded me of our first meeting with Paul from Immortal. Jeff and Pete said all of the right things. They totally got us. At the time they were running their management company out of Jeff's tiny living room—today, of course, they run The Firm, one of the largest management companies in the world where they handle only the best of the best in entertainment.

Even though they didn't have an office, we went with them. We knew it was the right choice from the moment we all met.

By the end of 1993, we had finished our first album and Korn was ready to go out on our first tour with Biohazard and House of Pain in the fall of 1994. Immortal gave us just enough money to buy an old, used RV to use as our "tour bus." That ride was a real jalopy. You could barely steer it when driving. It was so beat up. Jeff Creath agreed to come along as our official driver and tour manager, although we all agreed to share in the responsibility of driving cross-country.

Our first show was in Atlanta. It was a two-thousand-seat club. Most of the shows on this tour would be for crowds between fifteen hundred and three thousand people. To get to the gig, we had to drive from L.A., which took three or four days. We all took turns driving, which didn't really help things since everyone was partying so hard along the way. Two hours out of Southern California, the RV broke down. We got it rolling again, but two hours later, the thing caught fire. It caught fire nine times on that trip. Somewhere in the middle of Mississippi, I fell asleep at the wheel. I pulled over and tried to get one of the other guys to wake up and drive.

No one moved.

I started screaming, "You've got to get up! I can't drive!"

No luck, so I kept on driving because we had to be in Atlanta in time for the show. We were way behind schedule because the RV had broken down so many times along the way. And, to be completely honest, we hadn't really clued in on how to manage our time yet. We had never toured before. Life was one big party and the RV our party mobile.

We got to the venue around the same time the doors opened for our show. We missed our sound check and had no time to do a run-through. Biohazard's tour manager was already thinking of canceling our show. Somehow we were able to convince him to let us play. We hustled our equipment onto the stage with barely a minute to go before showtime. Just in case you don't know this, running late, missing a sound check, and not being where you're supposed to be on the night of your first show is never a good idea. Lucky for us, we rocked it.

We played our next show the following night. From that show through the rest of the tour, we were ridiculously prompt. When we did our first sound check of the tour, a couple of

Hanging out at
the listening party
at Indigo Ranch.

guys from Biohazard were checking us out. They were completely blown away. Biohazard kept their drums set up on the stage while we performed, so we had to set up in front of their equipment and monitors, leaving us barely a couple of inches in the front of the stage to perform our show. We literally had no room to move. We were used to jumping up and down and working the crowd. If I moved at all, I would have fallen off the stage. But we didn't complain. We were so happy to be on tour, it didn't matter where we played—as long as we were out there each and every night.

It took a little getting used to the fact that the crowds didn't care about us. We had every right to be pissed, because we were being treated like we were just some random opening act. They were there to see Biohazard and House of Pain. If a hundred people out of two thousand were booing us, flipping us off, and spitting at us, it felt like the whole crowd. We'd rip through our sets without taking a break so we didn't have to hear the crowd. We had a passion for what we were doing so we dutifully played our music and left the stage. Every now and then, the crowd would tune it, but the shows weren't what we were expecting. We played legendary venues such as the Fillmore in San Francisco and the Civic Auditorium in Santa Monica. We continued to play some smaller clubs along the way, too.

One of the things I remember well from that first tour was the beginning of my hard partying on the road. Jeff did his best to try and reel us in, but we were totally out of control.

Out on tour . . . and baked.

We all partied pretty hard, including Jeff, so it was hard for the shepherd to effectively herd his sheep. As I mentioned, at the time, several of the guys were doing a bunch of speed and drinking tons of beer. Taking amphetamines was more my thing when I was younger, but I never snorted them. I'd pop a pill or two every now and then, but they made me feel too anxious, so it was rare as I got older. I started becoming more hooked on the feeling I got from taking downers and my late-night binge eating was getting worse. If I was in a hotel room, I could make the perfect quesadillas using only an iron. I'd stop at a local 7-Eleven, grab some cheese and tortillas and fry those suckers with a steaming hot iron. If I was someplace where there was an oven, I could make the best tortilla pizza in less than twelve minutes. I'd grab a tortilla, spread pizza sauce all around it, toss a heaping handful of cheese on top and bam! Between the drinking and late-night eating, I was heavier than ever.

About halfway through that first tour, our RV finally kicked the bucket. We had to quickly find a van to use for the remaining three weeks of the tour. It was pure hell because it wasn't a tricked-out comfortable rock star van. It was more like an old used ten-passenger van you'd take to the airport. We'd sit in our seats, facing the row of seats in front of us trying to sleep in an upright position. It was horrible. There was a small cargo space in the back that we took turns rotating to so we could get some sleep in a reclining position. Getting that space was the highlight of traveling those last few weeks. It became totally unbearable. We were wrecked from partying, playing, and no sleep. Finally, we demanded a tour bus to finish the remainder of our time on the road. We threatened to quit unless Jeff found us a bus. He kept telling us we couldn't quit—that we had to finish the tour. We didn't care. We laid down our demand. Even though we couldn't really afford it, they some-how ended up finding us the cheapest bus to use until the end of the tour. Managers rock. They can make miracles happen and often do to keep their clients happy.

Something we didn't quite understand in those days was that everything you do while touring comes out of your own profits. The money spent on tour is like taking a loan from the record company. Ultimately, we pay for everything from meals to all of the expenses for the crew. Eventually, the money has to be paid back. We were young and naive. Plus, we were so certain we were going to be huge, we figured it didn't matter. We believed there would be plenty of money to pay our expenses and go around. It was an important lesson learned. We didn't make as much money on the first tour as we might have expected to, but we sure did learn a lot.

Almost immediately upon our return to Los Angeles, we played a few club dates up and down the California coast with the Deftones. We went back into the studio to record our second album, *Life Is Peachy,* before the end of the year. We asked Ross Robinson to once again produce. We knew we wanted to head back up to the Indigo Ranch because the first album turned out so great. We wanted that same energy and inspiration we found up in the Malibu hills. Even though I prefer to be closer to the city, the ranch was isolated and far away from everything that would distract us from doing some great work. We could party and record without any outside influences or temptations unless we invited it into our space. When we got bored or just needed to blow off a little steam, we would shoot some hoops on the beat-up cracked cement court that was in the parking lot. And though the accommodations were minimal and rustic, I found that I actually enjoyed being up there. I am sure I'd appreciate it a lot more today than I did back then because I have grown to love hiking and the outdoors. I was so grateful to be doing what I loved, it never occurred to me that things could (or should) be any different.

I came up with the title for the album *Life Is Peachy* from an old folder I used to bring to school called a *peachy*. For whatever reason, I always added in the words *Life Is . . .* in front of the printed word *Peachy* on the front of the folder. I thought it was funny. My favorite peachy folder was yellow with lots of printed funky characters on the front. I used to doodle all over it. I drew long hair on the characters and put guitars in their hands. I used to sketch stuff all the time. I eventually knew that my scribbles might someday pay off. I thought that visual would make a really cool album cover.

We contacted the company that makes the folders to see if they would give us permission to use the image for the cover of the new album. We offered them twenty thousand dollars for the rights, but they turned us down. Even so, we all agreed *Life Is Peachy* was a great name for the album, so we kept the name without the folder art.

It seemed like making *Life Is Peachy* all happened so quickly. Even the songs we played were fast. I think we were all excited because the first album was enormously successful, having sold more than 1 million albums and gone platinum. *Life Is Peachy* almost had a punk rock feel because the rhythms and drumming were so aggressive. We knew the sound we were going after so the overall experience was really smooth. Songs came flying out of us as if they were just waiting to be recorded.

We shot our first video for the album for "A.D.I.D.A.S." ("All Day I Dream About Sex") with Joseph Kahn, a very sought after director. It was one of the hardest videos we ever made because we had to lie still on cold metal slabs for hours, pretending to be dead. We wore weird dirty blue contacts in our eyes that made us practically blind while they were in. There was a guy on the set whose sole job was to wrangle flies that he somehow crippled, literally rendering them motionless for a minute or two so he could place them on our faces. I have no idea how he got the flies to stay still. His magical fly powers were bizarre.

We also hired actor John DeSantis who played Lurch in *The New Addams Family* to play a big crazy scary dude in the video. The premise of the video was that we were all killed in a car crash.

We closed off a tunnel in downtown Los Angeles for the shoot. The director created a spooky feel with fake rain all throughout the shoot. A lot of people thought the rain was real, but it wasn't. It was our first encounter with true Hollywood movie magic.

When they zipped me up in the body bag, I actually had a full-blown panic attack. It tripped me out so much that I threw up. At the time, everything gave me anxiety, but this was especially intense. I was an overweight drunk who was suddenly trapped in the confines of a body bag. That was enough to push me over the edge that particular day. It was nearly impossible to lie still while dealing with my panic and anxiety. It took every ounce of inner strength I had to get through that shoot. The video did turn out really cool. I think it is one of the most interesting we ever shot.

At the time, I was a huge Ice Cube fan, so I approached the guys with the idea of covering one of his songs called "Wicked." I wanted to get a surprise artist to come help us record it so I asked my good friend Jay Gordon from Orgy to come into the studio to rap Ice Cube's part while Jon sang the chorus. Orgy hadn't hit yet so no one outside of diehards knew who Jay was. We thought it would be a good idea to get someone with a recognized name to join in, too, so we asked Chino Moreno from the Deftones to help out. We had just played several club dates with the Deftones so we had a pretty good rapport with them. Chino said he already knew the song and was down with doing it.

When he and Jon got into the studio, it was crazy. They were both completely wasted, jumping all over the room while we tried to get a decent take. If you listen closely to the song, you can hear how trashed Chino was at the time. He is slurring his words on the track. After listening to the playback, though, we decided to leave it the way it was recorded because there was such a cool vibe there despite the drunken muttering. It turned out to be a really fun song.

Making *Life Is Peachy* happened in a quick blink. During those first few years of writing, recording, and touring, there was never any downtime—and I liked it that way. We were so excited about everything that was happening for us. We were like a bunch of little kids living out our wildest dreams. Everyone was so happy, we used to joke around saying we would have done it all for free. (Don't tell our record company.)

As soon as we finished recording we headed out on the Sick of It All Tour from January to March 1995. We were immediately asked to go on tour with Marilyn Manson and Danzig on the Danzig 4 Tour from March through May. There wasn't even a couple days' break in between the two tours. The Danzig 4 tour was one crazy experience. By the second week of that tour, our second album had dropped. While playing in Detroit, I received a call from Jeff and Pete to tell us *Life Is Peachy* debuted at number three on the Billboard charts, selling 106,000 copies in its first week. (We would go on to earn a Grammy nomination for best metal performance for the song, "No Place to Hide," and to date, that album has sold close to 3 million copies worldwide.) I was literally in tears when I heard the news. That was really cool. By the following week, they said we were selling 2,500 and then 3,500 albums the next week. Now we were outselling Manson and Danzig combined. Even our merchandise was selling better than theirs. We were the opening band outselling the featured artists. It was all happening so fast. It was crazy. People were definitely catching on to us. We could feel the growing energy at every show. Maybe Danzig and Manson could feel it, too.

Life on the road with Manson and Danzig was a nonstop party. Someone was always doing something. We could go from dressing room to dressing room backstage and check out what was going on. Occasionally Manson would come into our dressing room with a broken beer bottle in his hand.

"Hey, guys, watch this." And he'd proceed to put the rigid edge of the bottle to his chest and rip it through his skin.

I'd say, "Yeah, that's cool" but I never understood why he was doing that. The act didn't shock us. We couldn't have cared less.

One night I was on my bus after partying long after the show ended. I was completely wasted and ready to go to sleep. One of the tour managers from Marilyn Manson came out to wake me to tell me there was a big party at the hotel that I couldn't miss.

"Go away. I'm sleeping," I growled.

He said, "You have to come to this party. It's the biggest party of the tour."

I reluctantly got up and headed to the hotel across the parking lot from where our bus was parked. I took the elevator to the tenth floor, walked into the hotel room, and saw a bunch of guys from Manson and Danzig's crew. When I walked into the room, some guys hiding behind the door jumped out, grabbed me, threw me on the bed, and put my hands behind my back to handcuff me. They were all laughing and screaming, "Take his pants off!"

In my calmest Mafia voice I said, "If you take my pants off, I will come back with my friends and kill you. I am serious. I . . . *Will* . . . *Kill* . . . You."

Something must have clicked in with those guys that said I wasn't joking around because they suddenly took the handcuffs off and let me go. I stood in the room for a minute trying to play it cool like it didn't bother me, but I was pissed. I could feel how hot and red my face was. I was embarrassed and angry at the same time. I have no idea why they did that to me, but looking back I can guess it was because they were trying to call me out to see if I was as tough as I acted.

The entire tour was strange. I remember using a pay phone outside a venue one night before a show. I was mesmerized by the crowd going in. All I could think was, *Man, this is the ugliest crowd I have ever seen!* Everybody was wearing black and lots of makeup. They all looked so depressed. Goth was hardly the image we were going for. We wanted the fans who wore baggy pants and Adidas—not some Morticia Addams wannabes. I had my doubts that we belonged on that tour from the very beginning, but we were playing pretty big places, which made us feel like we were becoming a huge band.

Even though Korn had been out on several tours, I still wasn't making a lot of money. I had pretty much blown through my share of the advance money from our first and second albums. When we were off the road, I came home and

That's Mom in front of our tour bus.

had to go back to work cleaning carpets. It was still one of the only things I knew how to do other than playing bass. I was living in my tiny one-bedroom apartment I shared with Sidney in Huntington Beach that I paid around $600 a month for in rent. I was barely making enough money to cover that, so I did whatever I had to do. Shortly after the tour with Manson and Danzig, however, I finally got my first taste of success. The album went gold, and royalties started coming in, so I traded in my Mercedes 190 for an E320 bubble-eyed Benz. Even so, I couldn't help but feel that all I had to show for my hard work was a gold record on the wall and a $50,000 car.

Big deal, I thought.

I wanted more. I wanted a mansion, luxurious cars, and all of the trappings of my newfound life.

Even though I needed the money, when my managers came

to us to go on tour with Megadeth, I didn't want to do it. It felt wrong in every way. Megadeth was more heavy metal while we were a combination of sounds; I felt their genre didn't go with our style or match up with the fan base we wanted. Jeff and Pete said we'd be playing thirty-five-hundred- to five-thousand-seat venues, which would be the largest ever. Despite our concerns, they somehow managed to convince us it would be a good idea. They knew we could turn every single one of those fans into Korn fans. And . . . so did we.

We went on tour with Megadeth, Fear Factor, and Flotsam and Jetsam in the summer of 1995. Even though Jon played his bagpipes on our first album, this was the tour where he introduced them to audiences. Bagpipes and Megadeth fans go together about as well as peanut butter and mustard. The fans didn't want to hear anything but Megadeth. Every night, we'd get a bunch of "boos" that seemed to snowball into the entire venue telling us to get off the stage.

We didn't hang out with the other bands on that tour at all. I think there is a perception that bands that tour together are friends. For the most part, that was never the case with us. We kept things pretty friendly, but never did anything together before or after our shows. We'd all end up backstage after the shows, where we'd hang out, but we never really talked about anything special. There was never the type of exchange where we discussed the crowd or the performances. For the most part, it was a bunch of us sitting in a room or standing around with a drink in one hand while scoping out the girls to see what chick we would hunt down to bang for the night. It was fun, and it was all I knew. I wasn't looking to make friends or network with other musicians. Rock and roll is a business, and our job was to play for the crowds that came to hear our music. That was about the extent of the camaraderie among us, especially on that tour. Needless to say, it was a rough tour but we still managed to do whatever was necessary to get through it.

By this point, I had truly discovered the "sex, drugs, and rock-and-roll" life. Looking back, I can tell you that is by far one of the worst sayings of all time. It sounds like the coolest thing ever, but I wish someone had told me to be careful of the downside that comes with that world. I would have absolutely loved living that life if it didn't bring on severe anxiety attacks, overeating, and overindulgence in drugs and drinking.

My first marriage had disintegrated and by the time I was in the studio recording *Life Is Peachy,* I was dating a woman named Shela, who was married to Scott Ellis, a drummer I knew from the band Human Waste Project. I met Shela through Jeff Schartoff, a guy I knew from Huntington Beach who played bass for the band. He introduced me to Shela one night after a show. She was really short with superthin, straight bobbed hair she wore above her shoulders that framed her face around her jawline. She was cute with a dark complexion and brown eyes. Even though she told me she was married, we immediately hit it off. She came on to me pretty strong, almost telling me to ask her out. She wasn't acting slutty, but was definitely flirting with me in more than a friend way. I got her number on the down low and we started dating. She was already having marriage problems that came to a head when her husband discovered she and I were hanging out. She eventually got divorced, and like Sidney, Shela almost immediately began pressuring me into getting married. I was twenty-four years old. I had already been through one divorce. I wasn't ready to go down that path again. I was reluctant to commit to Shela, which frustrated her. I didn't care. Marriage was the last thing on my mind.

Korn and everything that came along with being in the band was all I cared about. I was leading the ultimate rock star life. If hot chicks wanted to come hang out, I was cool with that. It they didn't, that was fine, too. I spent countless nights messed up in strip clubs, throwing money around like I had it to spare—which I didn't—and pretending I was single. That was the image I had of how a big rock star should act.

I never went to strip clubs until Korn got a taste of fame. As strange as it sounds, I was rarely there for the dancers. I didn't like getting lap dances but I enjoyed the atmosphere of being in those clubs. It didn't matter what city we were in. Strip clubs are pretty much the same wherever you go.

Me with my second wife, Shela, in 1997.

Five to ten of us from the crew would usually go together. We'd all sit at a large table but never say a word to one another. All of the focus was on the girls or throwing back as much beer as we could get down. I spent those hours mostly looking around, listening to the music, and drinking—a lot. Being in the clubs was more like watching a music video to me than anything else. It was just entertainment.

I was never seduced by the attention the girls gave me because I knew that was part of their job. By the end of the night, however, we usually had a few girls lined up to come back and party with us on the bus or at our hotel where we could make our own private strip club. We'd turn the music up so loud, there was no way anyone could have a conversation, so it was an easy transition when the girls came back with us. Nothing was forced. We'd all party and have a good time. For whatever reason, I was slightly more comfortable with the girls dancing for me on the bus than I was in the club. And yes, I slept with a few dancers, but it wasn't because they were strippers. It was merely because they were there. I'd like to say that I've learned something from every experience I've been through over the years, but looking back, those nights in particular seem like such a waste. They did nothing for me but fill time. When I think about the girls I met in the strip clubs, I feel sad for them. Most were pretty messed up mentally. I think so many of them had a long history of abuse in their lives, and for the most part, they were all addicts of some kind.

I know some of their pain firsthand because I was such a mess myself. There were plenty of nights I was so trashed that I should have been tossed out of the clubs and into the street. I'm sure many of the dancers I met probably think I was as messed up as they were. And they'd be right. The only reason I got away with my behavior was because I was a "rock star."

The bigger the band got, the worse my attitude and ego were becoming. I became very demanding and felt uncharacteristically entitled.

We started our first European tour in September 1995. One of the band's first stops was in London to do a show in Nottingham. We landed at Heathrow Airport early in the morning. We were all helping with the luggage and equipment because we didn't have a lot of roadies yet. We usually made one of the drum techs push most of the equipment on a giant cart because we thought we had to act like we were the cool rock stars. For some reason, I ended up pushing the drum kit through the airport that day and the tech was just strolling along empty-handed. Something just snapped inside me. I pushed the drum kit right at the dude and said, "I don't know why I'm pushing this. I don't even play the drums! I'm the rock star, you're the tech. It's *your* job!"

He got pissed off at me and we began to argue. Before I knew it, we were pushing each other. Just as we were about to escalate into a full-blown brawl, the London police intervened. I looked up and noticed we were surrounded by four or five AK-47s cocked and ready for fire. These dudes don't mess around.

They escorted us to a holding area in the airport where they proceeded to interrogate us and even searched a couple of the roadies. I heard some of the guys had to endure a full cavity search. Luckily, I wasn't one of those guys. They didn't want to let us get on our next flight to Germany, where we were scheduled to play our first big festival concert. Although we didn't want to disappoint thirty thousand fans—which was probably one of the largest crowds we played back then— the police were unrelenting, and we missed the show.

Missing a planned tour date is never good. There was all

sorts of media speculation on what happened at Heathrow. We finally released a statement to the press explaining what went down. I later heard that the lead cop that day tried to get a job working security for our band. We had a two-word answer for him: Hell no.

As the band's popularity exploded, my ego got way out of check. Like I did that morning at Heathrow, I let my new-found fame go right to my head. No one was more important than me. The only time I was nice to fans was after our shows. Something about those fans seemed different to me. They came to see us play. They laid down their hard-earned cash to come see our show. I thought they deserved the respect of saying hello or signing a few autographs before getting on the bus to leave for the next town. Sometimes I'd even stop and talk, give away T-shirts, and spend a few minutes shaking hands. If, however, I was at the mall or in a restaurant and a fan tried to say hi, I was hardly ever nice. It wasn't so much what I would say, it was more my tone of voice, which implied "Get away from me. You're bothering me." I could make someone feel an inch tall in less than a second. Most of the time, people would just walk away. But every now and then, I heard about it.

I was once at a music trade show when a couple walked right up to me and said, "Screw you. We hate you. You treated our friend like dirt. All he wanted to do was shake your hand and you dissed him. Screw you!" I had no idea what they were even talking about. I did that so often, there was no way I would remember exactly who their friend was, let alone care.

Most of the time, I was so wasted I couldn't think straight about anything. My judgment was impaired and deep down inside, my spirit wasn't at rest. My conscience didn't allow me

Getting out some aggression onstage.

to live that lifestyle without paying a very high price. When you're living a wrong life, I'm convinced you can't get away with it. You can try and run from your conscience, but eventually, it catches up. My growing dependency on Xanax started as a way to get some sleep, but my need for Xanax grew to the point where I was taking it all day long as a way to drown out my ever-growing guilt. At the time, I thought I was taking it to get high. But now I realize, I couldn't cope with how I felt. The conscience never shuts off. The guiltier I felt, the more severe my panic and anxiety got. Plus, we were on the road all the time, which was increasingly hard for me.

I spent the bulk of 1995 to 1997 on the road, touring non-stop with bands such as Ozzy Osbourne, Sugar Ray, Life of Agony, Monster Magnet, Grotus, Cradle of Thorns, Metallica, Incubus, the Urge, and Dimestore Hoods. When we started touring in 1995, the band was being paid around fourteen grand a show, and by the end of 1997 we were making significantly more. When we hit the road alone for the first time, we went back and played the same places as we did with Megadeth, only this time, we were the headliners and were selling out night after night, doubling and even tripling the crowds we had touring with Megadeth. It was sweet retribution. We were coming up so fast. I loved every minute of it.

Success brought a lot of perks, especially when it came to partying. We were all drinking and using our various drugs of choice more than ever. Some bands out there really know how to handle their fame. We weren't one of them.

As an attempt to balance my excessive rock star life, I threw myself into music practically as hard as I was partying. I found an interest in discovering new artists and cultivating their talent. I first met Fred Durst in November 1995 outside of the Milk Bar, a small club we played in Jacksonville, Florida. He was waiting for me after the show. When I walked out of the club, he grabbed Head and me and said he wanted to talk to us. Fred said he was a tattoo artist and he'd do our tattoos for free. I was down with that. Today, my entire body is pretty covered in ink, but back then I still had lots of places I wanted done—and free was always a good price so it seemed like an excellent idea. Fred told us his studio was right down the street. I thought, *All right. Let's roll.*

On our way over, Fred started pushing a little more than tattoos, saying he had a demo tape of his band, Limp Bizkit, for me to listen to. I wasn't all that interested in hearing about his band so I kept talking about what kind of tattoo I should get. We finally got to his friend's house where there was a makeshift tattoo studio. Fred got all set up and wanted to know who was going first. Head said he'd go. Man, am I glad he said that. I watched as Fred attempted to tattoo "Korn" across Head's lower back. It was a simple design, something that should have taken a pro less than fifteen minutes. Four hours later . . . well, needless to say, I didn't really want to go next. It was getting late and I was pretty tired. We'd all been throwing back lots of Coors Light so I decided to go to the bathroom and fill my empty beer can with water so no one would know I wasn't drinking. (This didn't happen very often, but on this particular night I was just tired from our show and waiting around for so long.)

When I looked at the finished tattoo, I didn't want to be the guy who told Head that his tattoo looked more like "Horn" than "Korn."

Fred turned to me and said, "You ready?"

"Uh. . . You know what? It's getting kind of late. I'm going to fly but I'll come back and do it another day."

Free or not, there was no way I was letting Fred do a tattoo. Even so, Fred kept pushing his demo tape. He pleaded with us to listen to it, saying, "It's so phat." He was obviously pumped. I have to admit, he intrigued me by the way he described the rap-metal sound of Limp Bizkit. I thought it sounded really cool, like something I could actually get into, so I gave him a break and asked to hear what he had. I really liked what I heard. Their songs "Counterfeit," "Stuck," and "Pollution" were all on the tape. I told Fred that we were heading back to L.A. to record but he should definitely keep in touch.

I mentioned Fred and Limp Bizkit to Ross Robinson, our producer. I insisted he had to check them out. I was relentless in my attempts to convince Ross it would be worth his while. After hearing their tape, Ross was down with wanting to produce them. I told Ross I could get Fred to come by while we were recording. I didn't know it at the time, but Ross called Jeff Kwatinetz, my manager, and told him about Limp Bizkit and said he should come by to hear the tape too. When he heard it, Jeff didn't like it at all. He didn't get their sound and wasn't into their whole vibe. I thought he was completely wrong. I begged him to give these guys a shot, this one time, to take my word these guys were going to be big. After a lot of groveling, I finally convinced Jeff to at least meet them.

Fred and I had been talking back and forth a lot. I told him I thought I could get my managers to take the band on as a client, and they would be produced by Ross Robinson. I gave him my word that I would oversee the whole thing. With everyone onboard, it was time to bring Fred to California to meet everyone. I knew Limp Bizkit's music was good, but I also liked their whole look and vibe. I figured Jeff might "get it" if he met Fred face-to-face. All of the groundwork had been laid. I expected Fred to be psyched, but he wasn't. He told me that Wes Borland, his guitar player, had recently left the band and Fred was unsure about what to do. I didn't care about this dude who had left the band. I told Fred I could find ten guitarists to take his place. We had to take a shot. He agreed but said he really wanted me to produce Limp Bizkit. I was cool with that, though I knew Ross would need to stay involved. I told Fred to come up to the studio so we could start getting some songs together.

Fred rented a van and made the drive from Jacksonville, Florida, to California. Somewhere in Texas, the driver fell asleep and rolled the van, causing it to flip over and over. By the time the guys made it to the studio, they were all bashed up. Thankfully, no one was killed, but Fred was on crutches while the other guys were all bandaged up, wearing arm slings and casts from broken arms. I could hardly believe my eyes when I saw them—they looked like they'd been through a war. When I checked out the van, there was blood everywhere. I'm not even sure how they made it the rest of the trip but there they were. We were back at the Indigo Ranch laying down a few new tracks when Fred and the rest of the guys showed up. It was a tough sell convincing Jeff these broken-boned dudes could make great music, but somehow we did it.

Fred made arrangements to record at DJ Lethal's home studio. I knew DJ Lethal from his days of being in House of Pain, though he would later join Limp Bizkit. One night I began messing around on the stand-up bass he had in the corner of the studio, adding some bass lines to the song the guys were working on. It sounded hot. We ended up partying until it got really late. I realized that the ranch was a solid forty-five minutes away from where we were in the Hollywood Hills. My friend Jeffy had driven me to the studio and I needed him to take me back to Indigo. Even though we were wasted, I told Jeff we had to go. As he made his way down the windy roads of Laurel Canyon, Jeffy began to hot-rod a little. Laurel Canyon is a really winding road that cuts through a mountain leading from West Hollywood to the San Fernando Valley. The road can be pretty treacherous, especially at night. Sure enough, Jeffy hit a sharp turn and skidded out of control. We spun around and slammed into a tree on my side of the car. I was knocked out cold on impact. The air bags deployed, which probably saved our lives, but the car continued to slide down the canyon until it came to stop over a fire hydrant. When I came to, water was shooting straight up in the air and pouring into the car from underneath, filling it up.

I tried to get the door open, but it was stuck. I pushed as hard as I could until it finally gave way. Water came gushing out of the car as I staggered alongside the canyon road, trying to get my bearings and to snap out of shock from the impact. We were both still wasted and weren't quite sure what we should do. I didn't want to go to jail so I said, "Let's just walk."

We left the scene and started walking down the curvy canyon road in the black of night, hopeful that no one saw us crash. A car slowly approached us from behind. The people in it pulled over to see if we were okay. When they did, they recognized me and asked if they could give us a ride. They took us all the way back to Malibu. Thankfully, when Jeffy finally dealt with the police, they couldn't prove we were drunk, so neither of us faced charges.

I ended up paying the price for that error in judgment anyway. The next day, I could barely move my neck. It was painful to sneeze or cough. I wasn't sure if I had suffered any internal injuries, but my whole body felt like it had been jerked around on the inside. It took a solid year or two to get my body back to where I didn't feel any pain or discomfort from that night, which sucked because I am pretty aggressive when I play the bass, so performing during that time was pure agony.

Something told me that producing Limp Bizkit's album wasn't in the cards for me. Between those guys crashing their van and my crash with Jeffy, I decided it wasn't the right time. Nothing seemed to be working. Even so, Ross Robinson said he'd do it. And they were able to convince Wes to come back to the band so I knew they'd be okay.

Funny enough, I did end up getting a tattoo from Fred. While he was waiting for Limp Bizkit to really come together, Fred got a job working in a tattoo shop in Hollywood. With a little practice, he actually ended up doing pretty good work. I decided to have him tattoo "Korn" on my ankle. At the time, I really liked the font Kid Frost was using for his stuff so I had Fred use that same lettering for my tattoo.

As I predicted, Limp Bizkit ended up becoming a huge success, selling millions of albums worldwide. They toured with us when we promoted *Life Is Peachy,* but we lost touch after their first album came out. They were out touring nonstop and we were really busy as well.

Once Korn began taking off, I discovered one of the benefits of being in a famous band was something called *rock doctors.* Rock doctors are regular physicians who love rock-and-roll stars and who are more than willing to get them anything they ask for, such as Xanax, Valium, Somas, Kolonopins, and Ativan. Getting prescription drugs was easy.

One doctor, a dentist, even got me Emla, a numbing cream made with a mixture of Lidocaine and Prilocaine that is often used for burn victims. I asked for it so I could numb my skin before getting tattoos. This particular doctor would often come to shows with giant tanks of nitrous oxide. We'd sit around with giant balloons and get so high. Doing hits of nitrous was the closest feeling to death I have ever wanted to get. It made my whole body go numb, distorted my voice, making it sound really deep and rendered me completely immobile. It was literally impossible to think, move, or talk. You have no choice but to just be numb. Of all the drugs I ever did, I wish I had never done the nitrous. Although I've never done heroin, I've been told that doing it is similar in terms of feeling a lot of shame and guilt afterward. And even though I felt so bad when I did nitrous, I kept right on doing it. I'm not sure why people give in and do things they really don't want to do. I suppose it's because addicts are always chasing their next great high. I was no exception.

While a lot of people around me were smoking all the time, my drugs of choice were beer, pills, and food. I didn't start smoking weed until I was twenty-seven or twenty-eight.

And then, a friend of mine asked me if I wanted to get high. He could see how stressed out I had become. He brought a blunt over to my place and said, "Smoke this with me."

I was, like, all right. We smoked the whole thing.

"Roll another," I said.

That was the first time I smoked weed, and I smoked two whole blunts. I was extreme like that in everything I did, from playing bass to getting high.

Smoking pot became a daily habit. I actually thought I would drink less if I smoked. I always liked being the guy with the weed, so I kept a substantial stash of various types of pot at all times so I could supply my friends with whatever they wanted to smoke. After I quit selling pot, one of my best customers became a dealer and began supplying me with all of my herb. He became one of the biggest dealers around until things got kind of crazy with him. I heard some guys broke into his house, put a plastic bag over his head, and held a gun to his temple. Somehow he was able to talk his way out of being killed and eventually got out of the business.

By this time, I had become painfully aware that alcohol was slowly killing me. All I had to do was check myself out in the mirror to see that I was bloated and looked horrible. I had dark circles under my eyes and looked much older than I was. I was becoming unrecognizable to myself. Unfortu-

With my bass and a blunt.

nately, smoking pot didn't help me curtail my drinking. In fact, it got worse because now I was smoking, drinking, and popping pills. I had no internal struggle about whether to give in to that routine. It was downright easy.

I simply thought, *Well, now I can stay high all day long.*

I no longer had the desire to have a moment of sober time in my life. And since I started smoking, I no longer had to wait for night to catch a buzz. I could wake and bake, numb myself with pills, and drink until I passed out. The second I woke up in the morning, I'd take a bong rip. As soon as I could start to feel it wear off, I'd take another. And though there wasn't a lot of logic to my thinking, I successfully avoided drinking during the day by staying high. It was easy to bring pot or pills with me wherever I went during the day. It was a lot less convenient to drink, so I'd pop pills and smoke weed all day long until the early evening—that's when I'd start to drink.

One night Jonathan and I were getting really drunk. His drink of choice back then (he's now sober) was Jack Daniel's, so I called him "Jack O'clock" because we always knew when it was time for Jon to start drinking. He could suck down a bottle of Jack faster than anyone. One thing about Jon, when he drank, he'd bite. On this particular night, he bit me in the chest. We were both wasted. After he bit me, we began to argue until it got so escalated, it was about to become violent.

I put my fists up and said, "C'mon, let's go. Right here and now."

Jon did the same. "All right, let's fight." Now we both had our fists up.

I said, "C'mon, you punk. I'm sick of this. Bring it on." We were screaming at each other waiting to see who would have the courage to throw the first punch.

And then, we both just started laughing. We put our hands down and thought, *What are we doing?*

Neither of us could go through with it. But that was pretty much par for the course. Nights of hard drinking always ended up bad. I did things drunk I would never do sober. That's the biggest deception when it comes to drinking. You get a false sense of security and a fake dose of courage. I said things that would never come out of my mouth if I hadn't been drinking. And even though I didn't know it at the time (not that I would have cared much if I did), I hurt a lot of people along the way. I always had something degrading to say or some snide comment to bag on everyone around me. Mostly I did it to cause a scene. I was intentionally being antagonistic to bring attention to myself. I wasn't the most-liked person, but for some reason, everyone put up with me.

One night, Head, Munky, Jon, David, and I decided to see who could drink the most beer. To me, this contest was a slam dunk. We kept track of our consumption by writing a slash on the wall in the studio to represent each beer. When you got to five, you put a diagonal slash through the four single lines. When I got to thirty-two beers, I was done. Head kept going. I think he polished off somewhere around forty-five beers that night. It was ridiculous. To make matters worse, we were shotgunning beer bongs all night long. We pulled out this big funnel that we tied a hose to and poured a beer into it. When you were ready for the beer, you moved your thumb out of the way and the hose would shotgun the beer down your throat.

And with all of this partying, this internal rage and anger began to overtake me. I was brutal to everyone around me. For no reason, I'd say the meanest stuff. I'd tell people how stupid they were, I'd put them down, verbally abusing them worse than if I punched them in the face. My behavior was unpredictable so when someone would ask me if I needed anything before a show I could be nice or I might say something like, "If I f—in' *needed* something, I would f—in' ask you for it, dickhead. Why are you bugging me all the time? Don't f—ing ask me that anymore!"

It was unnecessarily aggressive considering they were only looking out for my best interest. While the words were harsh, my delivery wasn't meant to be. I'd usually try to mask my irritation by responding with more of a sarcastic tone than an angry one. But my language was so foul that most everything I said came off rude and obnoxious even if I tried to mask it with sarcasm. For a while, I could get by on that approach. But it wasn't long before everyone could see through that very thin veil.

The worst reactions of all usually came when we would run out of beer. I threw a tantrum every time. I'd threaten to fire everyone if they didn't get beer, "in the next five minutes."

I'd rant, "This is bullshit. If someone doesn't get me some beer right now, I am going to send you all home." And I meant it, too. I fired a lot of people over the years because of my short temper. If a bus driver went over too many bumps, I'd approach him while he was driving and say, "What the hell are you doing driving like that?" When we got to our destination, I'd get right on the phone and have the tour manager fire him.

I was pissed off all the time when things weren't perfect. Of course, today I realize nothing and no one is ever perfect. Things will and do go wrong. But I was just being the prick rock star who demanded perfection regardless of the consequences of my anger.

Sometimes, I'd get physically violent, too—especially after I'd been drinking. I was so volatile and unpredictable. No one knew when my tirades would occur, but they were all certain they would come.

One of my worst memories of being on the road was when I trashed my hotel room the night before a really big show. I was drinking, popping pills, and smoking weed. For whatever reason—I can't really pinpoint the trigger—I began destroying the room. I threw all of the plants, scratched the marble tables, destroyed the TV, and ripped all of the pictures off the walls. I threw empty beer bottles all over the room, watching them shatter into a million little pieces. It was chaos, exactly what you've heard about rock stars behaving badly. I'd never done it before or since. It cost me four grand to pay for the damages. Take my word—it wasn't worth it. What a waste of money!

The next day, I was really bad off. I couldn't stop dry heaving or shaking. I can't remember feeling worse than I did that day. Later that night, I got onstage and just stood there the entire show, still dry heaving, playing my bass and hoping I wasn't going to die.

Though I didn't know it at the time, I was living in the pit of hell. It had nothing to do with my fame. It had to do with my own ego believing this was appropriate behavior. But, I look at this time in my life like this: if I didn't have the history of my past, nobody would want to know about my future.

We come to this place, falling through
time living a hollow life.

Always we're taking, waiting
for signs, hollow life . . .

FROM "HOLLOW LIFE"

—KORN

In many ways, I was living a hollow life. From the outside looking in, I had it all. I was beginning to make money doing what I loved most—playing music. MTV was starting to play our videos and Korn was definitely headed for the big time.

Korn toured in the 1997 Lollapalooza summer tour. Jane's Addiction, Tool, Tricky, Snoop Dogg, Prodigy, and many others were on the road with us as well. I came up with the idea that Jon, Munky, and I should all come onstage riding lowrider bikes that had chain steering wheels and dingle balls around our seat. We parked them in front of our amps and left the bikes there the whole show. Jon and I built and customized the bikes from scratch.

That experience took my interest in customizing cars and bikes to new heights. From the time I got my first Toyota pickup truck back in high school, I always took great pride in my rides. Something about driving around in a tricked-out car has always made me feel cool. I'm a guy who has always liked old cars. I enjoy finding beaters and fixing them up by putting on chrome rims, custom grills, and adding hydraulics. I suppose it's another facet to my street style.

I recently bought a '64 Impala that I put air bags in—these aren't the safety type of air bags, but more similar to how hydraulics work, except they can lower the back, front, and sides of the car separately. I spent close to a year customizing the entire chassis, having it painted in this rich root beer metallic brown color. I had the convertible roof replaced with a fresh clean white vinyl that matched the white leather interior and added a steering wheel made from thick chain. Of course, I put in a bumpin' stereo system with a touch screen control panel. When I picked it up from the custom shop, it looked like a show car. I couldn't wait to strut my stuff in this bad boy. I put down the roof, cranked out some tunes, and made my way down the 405 Freeway from Westminster to Laguna.

On the way home, I noticed the car was starting to get hot, the heat coming from under the dashboard. I didn't think much of it. When I pulled off the exit to my house, I heard this loud "pop," like I had blown out a tire. I pulled over to the side of the road and got out to see what was happening and saw large plumes of white smoke coming from underneath the car.

My '64 Chevy Impala caught fire and burned up while I was driving it.
Man, I loved that car.

Just then, another car pulled up next to me and said, "Hey, man, it looks like your car is on fire under the hood."

I squatted down to check it out. He was right. The heat was so intense, the paint was bubbling up from the hood. All of a sudden thet whole front of the car burst into flames.

"Poof!"

I stood there sort of dumbfounded by the whole scene. Thankfully, I am now at a point in my life where I can appreciate that it was God's favor that I wasn't in the car driving when this happened. Ten years earlier, I am certain I would have been freaked out. Souped-up cars were important to me back in the day, even when money was tight. They were a status symbol, a sign of success. Today, they're just a hobby.

Anyway, I called the fire department and peacefully waited for them to come and put out the fire. I watched as the tires popped, the interior burned, and the blaring music faded to a wobbly silence. Now all I could hear was the cracking sound of my car burning while I hoped it didn't explode. I stared into the flames, knowing it was just a car. But I couldn't help letting my mind wander, thinking about what car I would get next.

Watching that car burn was a hard lesson to learn. Since I had no insurance, it was a total loss. I estimate the damages to be well over thirty grand. I will never again own wheels without having insurance on it. Even though I never found out the cause of the fire, I should have known better than to let myself get burned.

Shela and I were still dating in 1997. Somehow, between all of the tours and being on the road, I had gotten her pregnant. Munky unexpectedly fell ill with viral meningitis and was hospitalized in late August, forcing Korn to drop out of the rest of the Lollapalooza tour. We made the decision to cancel the rest of our appearances because we didn't think we could possibly find a suitable replacement for Munky while he recovered. Besides, the canceled shows allowed me to be home when Shela gave birth to our little girl, Sarina, on September 30, 1997. Since I didn't have to be back on the road, I was able to be around for the rest of the year.

After I discovered Limp Bizkit, we were getting demos from all sorts of bands looking for a recording contract. We decided to start our own Korn record label in 1997, called Elementree Records. I had a custom gold necklace made with Elementree's logo, a burning schoolhouse. I was really into blinged-out jewelry, so there were close to five hundred diamonds inlaid all around the necklace. I wore that necklace all the time.

The first group we signed to the label was Orgy whose debut album went platinum, which means their album sold a million copies. The second band we signed was Videodrone, who I ended up producing.

I first met the guys from Videodrone back in Bakersfield when they played in a band called Cradle of Thorns. They hung out with Korn from time to time. One day we got to talking. They were saying that they wanted to form a new band and start over. I had some time off so I offered to lend a hand producing a few songs. At the time, Korn was pretty hot, so they were excited about working together. I had never produced anything before, but I knew the sound they were going after and thought it would be cool to help bring it all together. I always had a passion to work with bands, to be an outside ear to their music. As a producer, I won't play on an album unless the band really wants me to. I think they need to find and develop their own sound. If I can contribute musically to enhance that sound, I will, but mostly I just want to be that set of ears listening for the magic in the music.

Most of the guys from Videodrone lived in Huntington Beach, about thirty minutes away from my house in Long Beach, so it was pretty convenient to work with them at their place. The five-piece band practiced in a tiny one-car garage, mostly at night. They lived in an apartment complex so we had to keep the noise way down. I went to listen to them and chilled with my ever-present large ice chest full of Coors Light, which had now become a fixture in my life. I dragged that ice chest everywhere I went, especially when I knew it would be a long night, so I was never without a beer.

There were plenty of nights I drank and drove. One night after being in the studio, I stopped at Taco Bell on my way back to Laguna. It wasn't a long drive, maybe thirty minutes or so, but I had been drinking a lot and thought some fast food would help sober me up. By now I had developed some pretty severe stomach issues, and eating Taco Bell was definitely not helping. I tried to take Tums or other antacids, but they didn't do much to alleviate my discomfort, so I learned to live with the pain. I failed to recognize it was the drinking that was causing me all of these problems in the first place.

Anyway, I got back on the highway, eating my burrito, and by the time I finished it, I was almost home. I exited onto the off ramp when I suddenly swerved and flew off the side of the road and landed in some heavy brush. I looked around to see if there were any cops or witnesses. Luckily, no one saw me, so I got away with it. There were so many nights I knew I didn't belong behind the wheel, but that never stopped me from driving drunk.

I can recall another night when I swerved and lost control of my car. I ran over several tall sprinklers and brush until I came to a stop. I was tossed around pretty good, but got out without a scratch. I managed to get the car back on the road and drove home like nothing ever happened. The very next day I was drinking and driving again. Man, it was so stupid. When I think about working with Videodrone on that first album, I can't believe I made it out alive.

We mixed the album at a studio in Hollywood. I don't really enjoy the mixing process so I didn't spend as much time on that element of the album as I did during the writing and recording. Even though we were all but done with the album, I still thought it needed a few more songs. I wanted to add some special guest appearances to give the album an extra push. At the time, I called on Fred Durst and DJ Lethal to come play a part on "Human Piñata," one of the songs that I thought turned out amazing. I asked Head to play guitar on "Power Tools for Girls" and Jonathan Davis to come lend a hand, too. Ty Elam, the lead vocalist for Videodrone, and Jonathan were in Sexart together, so Jon knew the guys even better than I did. It wasn't unusual to spot Jonathan wearing a Cradle of Thorns T-shirt over the years. He was a big fan and was totally down with recording, lending his vocals to "Ty Jonathan Down," a very dark but powerful tune. The record company loved the song so much, they greenlit a music video for it, which was pretty unusual for a new band.

I asked some other friends who played in a hip-hop Latin band called Psycho Realm to participate on the album, too. The band was started by two brothers, Jacken and Big Duke. B-Real from Cypress Hill saw the band play in downtown Los Angeles and was so impressed with what he heard, he wanted to join their band. At the time, Cypress Hill was really hot so B-Real brought a lot of attention to Psycho Realm when he joined them. Psycho Realm collaborated on "Pig in a Blanket."

Hanging out backstage with B-Real in my weed-head daze.

Not long after recording together, I remembering hearing the story about the night Big Duke was shot in a confrontation while trying to split up a fight at Tommy's Burger Stand in downtown Los Angeles; he was left permanently paralyzed from the neck down. It was tragic, happening about a month before the expected release of their second Psycho Realm album.

I lost touch with those guys over the years, but I occasionally see Jacken around Los Angeles. I heard Big Duke is writing books and doing well. I'll still rock their CDs from time to time. They definitely hold up.

By early 1998 we were back in the studio to record our third album, *Follow the Leader.* We loved the work we had done with Ross Robinson on the first two albums but thought it would be a good idea to work with another producer to see what else we could do creatively as a band. We decided to work collaboratively with Steve Thompson and Toby Wright. We documented the making of the album by streaming weekly episodes of KornTV on the Internet. Our managers and the guys in the band thought it would be cool to let our fans see what was going on behind the scenes and allow them to experience the making of one of our albums. Thursdays were referred to as "No Work Thursday" because we dedicated the entire day to KornTV. We still recorded at night, but we couldn't get as much done as on all the other days.

Several friends helped out on various tracks of the album, including Fred Durst, Ice Cube, Tre Hardson from Pharcyde, and Cheech Marin. At the time, because of my weed habit I was really into the Cheech and Chong movies. There was a song that Cheech and Chong did in one of their movies called "Earache My Eye" that caught my attention. It was kind of a heavy and goofy tune. I wanted to cover the song for the album as a hidden track. I thought it would be cool to shake things up a bit by having David play my bass and Jonathan on the drums. Cheech and I could sing vocals, going back and forth on every other line. The band was up for doing it. All we had to do was get Cheech onboard.

Our managers reached out to his people to see if he would be interested. He said he'd love to do it, his kids were big fans of Korn, and he happened to be coming to Los Angeles to tape an episode of celebrity *Jeopardy!* When Cheech came down to the studio, he was nothing like the guy I was expecting. He was clean shaven, without his trademark big mustache. When he spoke, he sounded eloquent and intelligent and nothing like the Mexican stoner I watched in all of his movies. I was totally blown away.

"I'm ready to go," Cheech said. He already knew the words so we started to record. He was a total pro.

When he got into the studio, I couldn't contain my laughter because he suddenly started talking like the guy I knew from the movies. It took a bunch of takes because everyone was out of their element, playing different instruments and me on vocals with Cheech. And there was an awful lot of joking around going on, too. It was a lot of fun. I really loved working with Cheech and would gladly do it again.

Meanwhile, despite my lack of monogamy and commitment throughout our relationship, Shela and I finally decided to get married in May 1998. Deep down I think she knew I wasn't that into it, but I thought it was important to do the right thing for our daughter, especially since Shela was once again pregnant and due with our second child in December.

Follow the Leader was released on August 18, 1998. It debuted number one on the Billboard charts, selling 268,000 copies the first week. The album contained two of our biggest singles including, "Got the Life" and "Freak on a Leash."

We went on the first Korn Kampaign Tour a couple days after the album dropped to promote *Follow the Leader.* That tour wasn't about playing venues. It was an autograph signing and radio promotion tour to promote the release of the album. It was set up similar to the way politicians travel when campaigning. We gave out promotional material that included pins and bumper stickers. Much like the politicians in Washington, we had a few things we wanted to say and we never get that chance when we're on the road playing. We chartered a Gulfstream G-4 private jet to make sure we could get from city to city without missing a scheduled appearance.

Kampaigning was a great way for us to interact with our fans—something we can't do as well when we do straight in-store signings or promotional stops. The fans seemed to lap it up. We held mock "press conferences" where the fans could ask us questions about anything. No topic was off-limits. For the most part, they wanted to know all about the new album, why we didn't work with Ross Robinson this time around, and how to get their demos to our record label.

One of the most memorable stops on the tour was in New York City. We had arranged for a school bus packed with radio contest winners who all came with us for our first appearance on MTV's *TRL (Total Request Live).* The bus was equipped with smog machines so there would be smoke coming out of the windows of the bus. We had the sickest sound system installed, louder than any stereo I had ever heard blasting music from the album. Security rushed us through the huge crowd that gathered outside the *TRL* studio. Up to that point, my experience with *TRL* was watching the Backstreet Boys, *NSYNC, and the Spice Girls receive the kind of response we were getting that day. I didn't get the full scope of what was happening. Those groups were so mainstream and we were so heavy. The response and adulation we were receiving didn't feel real. How was it possible that Korn was suddenly fitting in with these types of bands? It seemed like someone was playing a giant practical joke on us. When we rolled up to the *TRL* studio, people were outside the studio flipping out, screaming and trying to get to us just like they did those other groups. Even though I knew we were becoming successful, I never realized that we were actually *popular.*

When we left *TRL,* we headed across the street to Tower Records to do a signing and hold a campaign meeting there. There was a huge, what appeared to be a never-ending line of people winding down Broadway waiting to see us. After the first hour, the New York City Police Department showed up to escort us out of the city. One of the officers told me that the Spice Girls had been in town the week before us and didn't get half the crowd we got. They explained that our appearance was causing too much of a disturbance in the city and that we had to leave. They could have just chosen to shut down the signing, but they were afraid the same chaos would follow us wherever we went, so we did the only thing we could do. We obliged and left. That was one of the only times I can remember over the years where we didn't stay to sign every single autograph. Even so, we made sure that everyone got presigned posters and CDs so no one left empty-handed.

Korn made a commitment early on that we would never turn away a fan. I made it a point to make sure my signature was always legible, even when I was too wasted to know what I was signing. On this particular tour, we'd sometimes stay for hours to make sure no one was left out. Occasionally I'd begin to nod off, with my head lying on the table while I scribbled my name over and over again. Even if I was wasted, except for that appearance in New York, I always stayed to the bitter end.

The cops in New York were being extra cautious when they asked us to leave, but there had been one city on that tour where the fans got so out of control that a miniriot occurred among the hundreds of fans who showed up. While we were doing short Q&As, we suddenly heard a group of fans yell out. "This radio station sucks. They don't even play your music!"

Needless to say, we were stunned, but weren't sure what to do. One of us shouted back, "Well, why don't you tell them to play it?"

Before we knew what was happening, a small but enthusiastic group of fans had surrounded the radio station van that was in the parking lot and begun to shake it until they tipped it over. I don't believe anyone was hurt in the incident but things did get crazy. It was complete chaos. Police came to clear out the crowds and escorted us out of yet another city.

We left New York and headed to Toronto, where we were somehow able to arrange for the Canadian army to loan us a tank and let us ride on top of it down one of the main city streets. A large van followed behind with a huge sound system that blared "Children of the Korn" from our new album for everyone to hear. There must have been two thousand or more people on the streets that day. I couldn't quite grasp what was happening. Every signing was pretty much the same—chaotic, frenetic, and really fun.

While making *Follow the Leader,* the band knew there was something special about the song "Got the Life." We used to make fun of the song because Jon said it reminded him of something you might hear at raves, which were very popular

With Tre from Pharcyde trying to see which one of our deodorants works better.

at the time. But for whatever reason, we all liked the song de-spite the fact we thought our fans wouldn't embrace it. When-ever we played the new songs for friends, the record company, our managers, everyone singled out "Got the Life," saying it was the song they loved the most. It was unanimously decided that it would be our first single and that we would shoot a music video for it.

At the time, I was still driving my bubble-eye Benz. I came up with a concept for the video where I would give my car away to a bum. I thought Tre from Pharcyde could play the bum. I wanted to blow up cars and other fancy material things in the video as a way to show that we didn't care about those things. We could end the video with a shot of a big backyard party with all of our friends. In addition, I wanted to put two lowrider bikes in the scene and make it look like we were all down in Mexico, partying and having a good time.

Our managers suggested getting ahold of Joseph Kahn,

who worked with us on the "A.D.I.D.A.S." video. When they reached him, we decided to have a conference call with all of the band members so I could explain my idea for the video to everyone.

"That's the stupidest idea I've ever heard," Joseph said. He went on to tell us *his* thoughts on what *he* thought the video should be. As we listened, I looked at the other guys. Without exchanging a word, I could tell that we were all in agreement, so I picked up the receiver and hung up on Joseph.

The hairdo I rocked for the "Freak on a Leash" music video—1998.

We ended up hiring the very talented director McG to do the "Got the Life" music video. Unlike Joseph Kahn, McG was happy to direct the video using our vision. That video became the very first video in history to be retired on MTV. The executives from *TRL* said that "Got the Life" was the number one requested video for too long so they had to stop airing it so other artists would have a chance at the coveted number one spot.

Our second music video from that album, "Freak on a Leash," was nominated for nine MTV Video Music Awards, eventually winning for Best Rock Video and Best Editing. That video along with "Falling Away from Me" and "Make Me Bad," all songs from *Follow the Leader,* were also eventually retired from the MTV rotation. *Follow the Leader* sold more than five million albums, making it one of our biggest ever.

By the fall of 1998, we put together our own Lollapa-looza tour, with a bunch of our good friends, and called it our Family Values Tour. We came up with the name Family Values because so many of our friends who were like family to us played in bands. The twenty-seven-date trek, which ran from September 22 to October 31, grossed more than $6.4 million. We purposely kept the ticket prices under thirty dollars so the show was affordable to almost everyone.

Funny enough, Limp Bizkit ended up playing the first Family Values Tour in 1998 along with Ice Cube, Orgy, Incubus, and Rammstein. It was great to reconnect with Fred and the rest of the band. This was, by far, my favorite tour we ever did.

We put together a huge circular stage that rotated for the tour. The opening band was Orgy, and while they were on, Rammstein, the next band could get ready behind them. At the end of every set, the stage would rotate bringing the following act to the front. We hired C-Minus, a deejay from Power 106, an L.A. radio station, to spin records for the ten or so minutes it took for the next band to get ready. Limp Bizkit usually played next and then Ice Cube. Finally, it was time for Korn. The show was a nonstop music extravaganza.

Every band had its own outrageous sets. Limp Bizkit had two huge UFO-looking spaceships on stage and lots of space-age-looking props all over the stage. Rammstein did a lot of pyrotechnics, including a stunt where they shot fire out of their mouths. Orgy used a lot of neon lights, which was all they could afford as a band just starting out. Thankfully, they went first, so the audience probably didn't notice how lame their effects were until after the show.

Ice Cube and me sharing a beverage during the first Family Values Tour in 1999.

Finally, Korn had a two-story cage set up where contest winners from every city stood inside throughout the show. I often thought of unique ideas for staging our shows and pitched my ideas to the guys. This was one of my favorites. We had done a lot of shows where we used cages—some looked like jails while others looked like giant watchtowers. This prison theme was our most elaborate setup. We had two double-decker cages behind us on either side of the stage. We used a police siren to start the show while giant spotlights searched the crowd like an inmate had escaped from a high-security prison yard. We piped in helicopter sounds to give it that South Central L.A. feel and let the adrenaline build before we hit our first note. When I presented the idea to the other members of the band, they were sold. Even so, I still felt compelled to keep selling it to them.

"You don't have to telemarket it, Fieldy! We like it!"

I'm the type of guy that can keep selling even after I've

closed the deal. You've got to push ideas in this world if you want people to listen. Doors don't automatically open and opportunities don't just happen. You have to go out there and create them. And even though we all had an equal vote in the band, it had to be unanimous for anything to be approved.

The Family Values Tour was an enormous success, catapulting all of us to superstar status. It definitely put Korn firmly on the map as one of the biggest rock bands of all time. Our album sales skyrocketed, and for the first time, I felt like we had truly hit it big.

Within days of ending the Family Values Tour, my second daughter, Olivia was born on December 9, 1998. I was really excited to have another daughter. I wanted Sarina to have a little sister to have as her best friend. I am really emotional when it comes to these types of things and watching my daughters being born was extremely moving. Even though she was a perfect baby, Olivia had one small complication with a clogged tear duct. It took three months of constant attention and care, massaging her eye and giving her doses of her eye cream to heal her, but I was happy to do it. When it comes to my kids' health and well-being, I always make the time so I can be sure they get whatever they need.

Even though I was able to be home for her birth, it wasn't long before I would be back in the studio recording our fourth album and out on the road once again touring to promote *Issues*.

I was truly living my dream: I had a wife, two beautiful kids, all of the material things expected of a rock star—several cars, a beautiful home, and what appeared to be a great life. It seemed like things kept getting better as time marched on.

When we were asked to play Woodstock on July 23, 1999, I wasn't really sure what to expect. We were told it was going to be a really big show with something like 350,000 people expected to attend. We chartered a private jet with Limp Bizkit and flew to New York the day of the show.

When we got there, our dressing room was a solid football field away from the stage. Prior to going on, we could hear the fans chanting, "WE WANT KORN" over and over again. I had never heard anything like it. It was so overwhelming that it actually made me nervous. The crowd was getting somewhat out of control, throwing beer bottles and getting into fights because they wanted us onstage.

I thought it would be a pretty good night when someone told us just minutes before the show that a girl with "Korn" painted across her bare chest was hoisted onto some guy's shoulders in front of the stage. When we finally started to play, looking out on the crowd, it looked like endless heads of people. As soon as we started playing, everyone started jumping up and down. From my perspective, it looked like giant waves over the ocean. I later found out that because the crowd was so big, each section was hearing the sound a nanosecond later than the group in front, causing that rhythmic wavy sensation. It was trippy.

We opened with "Blind," which sent the crowd into an absolute frenzy. Someone set off fireworks just as Jonathan screamed his trademark, *"Are you ready?"* Although we didn't coordinate it, the fireworks were perfectly timed to the music and were a sight I'll never forget. We played our set, which included "Twist," "Got the Life," "A.D.I.D.A.S.," "Freak on a Leash," "Shoots and Ladders," "Faget," and a bagpipe solo by Jonathan, which had now become a staple in all of our shows.

At the end of the show, we all hugged it out and cried. I'm not sure if it was the venue, the crowd, or the energy that filled air that night that brought out that type of emotion in us. We have never been the type of band to embrace at the end of a show, but something magical happened that night. There was a lot of love between us that circumvented any negativity that may have penetrated the group over the past few years. There had been a building distaste among all of us. I think it was as simple as all of us just trying to find our own way with dealing with our success and fame. I was probably responsible for the vast majority of the hard feelings that had developed. I was living under a dark cloud, and I wanted everyone around me to pile in underneath it with me. I fed off all of the negativity. I found it so easy to rip people apart—even people I genuinely loved and cared for. At the time, I didn't understand that it is so much better to build someone up than it is to tear them down. Words can be as hurtful as physical violence. In that respect, I was a verbal Mike Tyson.

I never realized that I was causing harm because whenever I would start ripping on someone, other people would join right in. It gave me the false sense that I was just saying what everyone else was thinking. I can't remember a single time that one of the guys stood up and said, "That's not cool." In retrospect, it was totally uncool. It took me years to figure that out.

But something happened onstage that night at Woodstock that gave us back the bond we once shared. I can truly say that it was one of the most memorable performances of our career, one that I will always appreciate for what it gave us far beyond the performance.

Not long after Woodstock, Jon's grandfather passed away. He had to leave the tour to attend the funeral. By the time he got back, he had taken the necessary steps to get sober. I think when something dramatic happens in an addict's life, such as the loss of a loved one, or some type of humbling—a bring-you-to-your knees type of experience—something happens to change your perspective. Those events seem to be an opportunity to flip your life. I wish it didn't take a tragedy for most of us to seize that chance, but it does. Jon used his grandfather's death to turn his life around and has been sober ever since.

His choice to get clean changed the vibe in the band for the better. He has the most incredible voice, and once he started singing without being high, drunk, or hungover, his voice got even better. You could hear him more clearly and the tone was much stronger and more powerful than ever before. The quality of his performances greatly improved because he no longer had to cancel shows or force his way through because he was too sick to go on.

By 2000, the band was succeeding beyond my wildest dreams, but the reality in my personal life was that my second marriage was miserably failing. I was never home with my daughters because I was touring nonstop. And my substance abuse was getting so out of control that I was unbearable to be around. When I did come home, it was always brief, usually no longer than a week or two in between tours. I was exhausted and, mostly, just wanted to sleep. To make things worse, when I wasn't sleeping, I was always wasted, which meant my wife and I were constantly fighting. There were plenty of nights where I became brutally abusive, both physically and verbally, though my verbal attacks were far more common and, in many ways, more hurtful. I wasn't really against marriage, but I was in no state of mind to be in it, either. I felt pressured all the time. My inability to be faithful and my lack of desire to be sober were the ultimate one-two punch that eventually ended our marriage.

To be certain, I wasn't a very good husband, but then again, I never really learned how. My father wasn't the ideal role model growing up. I never learned how to love anyone else except myself. I didn't know how to love in the way Shela wanted or needed me to.

Once Shela and I had kids, I no longer slept in the same bed with my wife. It wasn't that I didn't want to be around her; I just didn't want to hear the kids at night. I was home for such limited amounts of time that my priority was catching up on my sleep. I was completely selfish. I am certainly not proud of this but it is the way things were. I thank God every day my daughters were too young to really know how messed up their dad was back then. They don't have any recollection of me being that way today.

Double-fisting beer was pretty typical for me back in the day.

Drugs and alcohol were my trusty and loyal companions. I was the Lone Ranger and they were Silver and Tonto. It had been so long since I felt . . . anything. I wouldn't even have recognized myself sober. I only felt like myself when I was drunk or high. I was like a walking zombie. That's how wasted I was all the time. And because I was numb, there was absolutely no communication going on with my wife. I didn't want to talk about anything—ever. I just wanted to drink and get high. That doesn't make for a very good marriage. I was young and foolish, and I often refer to my twenties as my terrible twos. It was all about me and there was no room, let alone desire on my part, to make my life about anyone or anything else.

And, if my absence wasn't hard enough for my family, my disrespect for my wife was unforgivable. I was never faithful in my past relationships. All throughout my marriage, my infidelity was by far the worst it had ever been. Once my career took off, the temptation of other women surrounded me like my own skin. I couldn't escape it—and even if I could, I didn't want to.

Out on tour with Papa Roach. Hangin' with Tobin Esperance at a preparty on my tour bus.

I suppose it was a godsend that I was on tour a lot more than I was at home. To be perfectly honest, I preferred it that way. I had as many women as I wanted, anytime, anyplace. I didn't have to answer for my actions and I could stay high 24/7. I thought I was living the life. I loved being in the number one rock band in the world. And I couldn't wait to be away from the pull of home and family.

Life on the road was so much easier for me, even when it was hard. I lived on my tour bus, my safe bubble and bastion of bad behavior. My bus was home, a haven where no one could touch me unless I invited them into my den of debauchery . . . or so I thought.

One night in Denver, several cops came knocking on my bus door. Like any night on the road, I was having a small party.

"You can't come walking in here. This is *my* bus!" I went into an immediate rage. Cops had never been on my bus and I was in no mood to deal with them on this particular night.

"Oh yes we can." They were not pleased with my aggressiveness or bravado. Their arrogance was infuriating.

"This is private property. This is my house. Get out of here."

Needless to say, there wasn't a lot I could do that was going to make them turn around and leave. I kept right on with my rant as they continued to ignore me. There were plenty of drugs around, mostly pot, but the cops didn't seem all that interested. The more I protested, the angrier they got.

"Keep it up, rock star. We'll haul you off to jail."

"You can't take me to jail. I'm in Korn. I'm in the biggest band in the country. You can't do a thing to me!" I really believed what I was saying. I truly thought I was invincible. The joke was on me because the next thing I felt was the stiff cold metal from someone's handcuffs being slapped around my wrists. I was actually being arrested.

The cops sat me in their patrol car while they finished searching the bus. I was screwed.

As I sat in the backseat of the car I noticed all of their paperwork on the floor in the front. I don't know why, but I somehow reached my foot under the seat and ripped it up with my shoe. While I was doing this the officer came back to the car and saw what I was up to. He reached in the backseat, grabbed me by the back of my neck, and threw me in the front of the car.

I looked over at the cop and said, "You're just mad at me because I make more money than you do." I went off on him, bad-mouthing the dude to no end.

"Keep it up, wise guy." He never reacted to one of my taunts, which was quite a remarkable feat because I could be very cutting. I could push anyone's buttons in a matter of seconds. But this guy had nerves of steel. Still, I tried.

"You're just sad because you have a sucky job and I'm a rock star who has it all." I kept going on and on while he continued to stay cool.

"Whatever." As hard as I tried, that was the biggest reaction I got out of him all night.

When we got to the jail, they threw me into a cell with thirty rough-looking guys. I walked in with my head down and my hands cuffed. I stared at the ground so I wouldn't make eye contact with anyone. I sat on the cold cement bench for hours. As soon as my body started coming down from all of my drinking and drugs, I climbed underneath the bench so no one could see me shaking.

I'll admit it, I was scared.

I was also detoxing.

I didn't want anyone to see me so vulnerable—not the cops or the other jailbirds—because then they'd know I was weak and that could have been a dangerous situation for me.

A few hours later, an officer came to take me to another cell. The new cell only had five other guys in there. You might have thought that fewer guys around would have somehow made this more tolerable for me, but it didn't. For whatever reason, I was terrified. Granted, I was in jail—and that alone is a scary place. But the dudes in this new cell were gnarly looking. I was truly panicked.

A few hours later, officers once again came to take me to yet another location. They placed me in between two glass sliding doors where there was a five-by-five space in between.

"Wait right here." They left me in that tiny space for three hours. I wasn't sure if they were messing with me but by this point, I was completely freaking out. I felt awful. My body was still shaking and my nerves were shot. It was everything I could do to resist puking.

Man, there I was in jail, and I wasn't certain I'd be able to make bail or if anyone really knew where I was. After several hours, my panic slowly began turning into humility. Somewhere in that three-hour span of isolation, I realized I was not in control. Being a rock star meant nothing in this place. By the time they took me to my final cell, I was truly humbled.

They sat me in a cell with the worst-smelling man I had ever met. His socks looked like he hadn't changed them for a year. He told me he was in for murder. By now, it didn't faze me a bit. We sat and talked like old friends, although I never looked him in the eyes . . . just in case.

When I was finally able to use the phone, I couldn't remember anyone's number at first. I took a deep breath to gain my composure and then somehow reached a friend of mine in L.A. who said there was nothing he could do to help me. I asked him to reach Jeff Kwatinetz and Pete Katsis. He said he'd try.

A solid twenty-four hours had now gone by and I wasn't even sure what I was in for. No one told me the exact charges or why they were holding me in the first place. I was pretty intoxicated when they brought me in. I was certain it wasn't for mouthing off to the cop. They must have found my stash on the bus. That was the only logical explanation. My mind was racing with all of the possibilities. It was a horrible way to pass the time.

I had only been to jail one trip prior to this night. My sister Mandi and I had been partying back in the day at a bar in Huntington Beach. Toward the end of the night, she got into an argument with a huge woman. This girl was triple the size of my sister.

Before I really knew what was happening, my sister turned to me and said, "Here, hold my purse."

Suddenly, she was on the ground with this large woman beating her head into the cement floor of the club. I didn't know what to do. I was so wasted, I wasn't even sure what I was seeing was real. A crowd began to gather around, and I realized I needed to do something. I took my sister's purse and began whacking it against this other girl's head. The next thing I know, this dude grabbed me from behind and hit me full force in the jaw. My good friend Tito Ortiz, the ultimate fighter, was there and saw what was happening. He jumped in. He flew through the air, did a spin, and kicked the dude in the jaw. Tito dropped that guy hard.

In the meantime, I had somehow unscrewed the metal

handle from a hose that was behind the bar. I was going to beat the guy in the face with it. Just as I was getting ready to bash him, the cops showed up. Thankfully, they didn't see what I was about to do. I was able to drop the metal handle before I could be arrested for something serious. Even so, the cops arrested everyone who was involved in the fight. I spent the night in jail, mostly sleeping off my buzz. I was released the next day with no charges brought against me. I'll never forget how I felt when they said I could go. And now, here I was again. Waiting and waiting—uncertain of when or if I would be set free.

"Reggie Arvizu." That's my given name. No one calls me Reggie except my mom and now the authoritative voice I heard calling me.

"Come with me," he said.

I followed the cop to his desk.

"Mr. Arvizu, we are charging you with molesting a cat."

I was in total shock. "What are you talking about?" I asked. "That has to be wrong."

"Well, Mr. Arvizu, there's not much I can do about this. It's on your paperwork. Looks like you're going to be doing some time with us."

I didn't know what to do. It was the craziest thing I've ever heard. Just as I started to plead my case, trying to explain that I had a show to do that night that I couldn't miss, the cop said, "I'm just kidding. You've been bailed out."

It turns out my managers had bailed me out hours before. It took nearly thirty-six hours to process the paperwork before they'd let me go. I was released just in time to make it from the jail to the concert. I was so pumped up from being free that I played an awesome show that night.

Fearing to fall and still the ground below me calls, falling down this time

Ripping apart all these things I have tried to stop falling all this time . . .

FROM "HOLLOW LIFE"

—KORN

I came home after touring for *Issues* to discover Shela had become a Jehovah's Witness. I respected that she was studying the Bible and learning about Jesus and God, but her newfound faith didn't fit into my lifestyle. Instinctively, I could tell that what she was into was real. I was still partying and doing my own thing, though, so I didn't want to know where her head was at. Something told me if I opened myself up to knowing about God my life would be forever changed. And I wasn't ready to give up the life I was living.

In her quest for complete disclosure and honesty in our relationship, Shela asked me if I was being right with her in our marriage. What she was really asking was whether or not I had ever cheated on her. I could tell she needed to know the truth. Maybe I also realized confessing the truth was my ticket out. I had been cheating on Shela from the second we met. That was who I was, and I never claimed to be any other way. Shela told me she needed to know the truth because if I had been unrighteous, she couldn't be married to me anymore. The way she worded her questions made it possible for me to let go without having to come clean. It also made it somehow easier for her to walk away with her dignity. I always appreciated how she handled that moment of truth because in the end, it set us both free.

By January 2001, it had become painfully obvious to both

of us that I knew our three-year marriage was finally over. Before it hurt our children, it was time to make our break. I left our new home in Laguna Hills that we moved into in 2000 and moved back into a second house I owned in Long Beach. The Long Beach house was the first real home I owned once I had a little money and was by far one of my most prized possessions. Shela and I lived in the Long Beach house for nearly six years before moving our family to Laguna Hills. I held on to the Long Beach place after buying our home in Laguna as an investment, but subconsciously, it may have been for other reasons, too. Even though it wasn't fancy or big, it was definitely a place where I felt safe and comfortable. Besides, I thought Shela and the girls would be happier in the bigger house. It turned out Laguna was just too big for Shela and, I'm only guessing, too painful for her to stay in. I bought her out of the house and moved back to Laguna by myself.

Shela was really easygoing about custody and visitation with the kids. She understood that my schedule was sporadic and unpredictable, so it was never a struggle when I wanted to see my daughters. In fact, we fought a lot less after our divorce than we did while married. I watched some of the other guys in the band suffer through really difficult divorces. They went through pure hell. I didn't want to do that with Shela. I pretty much gave her what she wanted and she did the same for me.

Our divorce was final by November 2001. After everything was resolved, I poured myself into work. Korn was back in the studio recording *Untouchables*. My drinking had hit an all-time high as well. It got to the point where we'd earmark a budget of $25,000 for pallets of Coors Light—and that didn't even include any hard alcohol we brought in while record-

Throwing up my own sign.

ing. This excessive drinking started while making *Follow the Leader* and continued to get worse as time went by. I spent all day at the studio, drinking from the moment I got there until we left at night. Friends would come and go throughout the day, and occasionally other bands, like the guys from Orgy, would stop by to hear us play.

If there wasn't beer at the studio, I wasn't showing up. That was one of my infamous "Fieldy's Rules." And when I say beer, I meant enough so I never had to worry about running out. This was as true on the road as it was in the studio. I'm sure you've heard stories about how celebrities make all sorts of outrageous demands for their dressing rooms. Well, our contract called for a certain amount of beer to be in the dressing rooms, on our buses, and in another room we called the "Chickenhead Room," aka the hospitality room backstage. It was where all of the groupies would go after the show.

Groupies would get invited to the Chickenhead Room by a couple of my guys who would go out into the audience and round up all of the pretty girls. They had it down to a science, too. We'd roll into an arena while they'd stroll the crowd and hand out backstage passes to girls they knew I'd "like." I didn't have a specific type. I just needed to get off. I was a lot like a lion in his kingdom. I'd hop on anyone. It didn't mean anything to me at all. I was conditioned to believe that the more women I slept with, the bigger stud I was. I even wrote some lyrics for my solo album, *Fieldy's Dreams,* about it:

> The more the fellas get laid
> The more that we're praised
> If a woman gets ██████
> Reputation of a slut
> Doesn't that suck?
> I didn't make the rules
> This is how it is
> In the world that we live

Of course, at the time, I didn't realize there would be a price to pay for that way of thinking.

After the concert, the girls sat in a certain section of the arena until it was time to herd them backstage like cattle to the slaughter. When the room was full, the guys would come and tell us we were all set. They'd have music playing, the lights were dimmed, and the mood was like a small and intimate club.

Whenever we wanted to bring the party back to the bus . . . we did. And I did practically every night on tour. If I didn't feel like making the short walk to the Chickenhead Room, I sent my personal "selector" (usually my assistant or one of the roadies) to pick out a few girls for me and bring them back to my bus. He'd come back and tell me the bus was stocked. That way I didn't have to waste my time going to the Chickenhead Room. I could just go back to the bus.

I was always careful to practice safe sex—mostly because I didn't want any unexpected surprises like kids or a nasty disease. I kept a whole drawerful of condoms on the bus. In fact, there was a wardrobe case packed full to get all of us through the tour. If we ran low, one of the guys made sure to restock before the next show. When I was done, I slipped off the bus, grabbed one of the guys, and told him to get rid of the girls. They'd oblige by going to the bus and simply announcing, "You ladies have to go. Get out." They were that blunt and abrupt. They'd literally kick them out.

After a particular show in Oregon, one of the girls actually refused to leave. She desperately wanted to ride the bus with me. I never liked any of those women hanging around after I was done. Occasionally, I'd let a girl or two stay on the bus for a minute—let them think they were going to ride with me and then kick them off. It was cruel, I know, but at the time it seemed sort of funny. I once shoved a girl out the door while the bus was pulling away. Some crazy legal drama went down after that particular night, so I never did that again.

Every now and then we'd have to pull out before I was through entertaining, so I'd let the girls ride along until we got to the first truck stop. I'd drop these girls in the middle of nowhere or make them get on the crew bus, which was not ideal for the girls because the crew would rotate them around until they were done and then drop them off at the next stop. This tour marked the beginning of a new game we'd play, which messed with these girls in the worst way. If for some reason a girl actually made it to the next city, we would give the guy a hard time about it, saying, "I can't believe you let her stay."

Even though there were hundreds of women over the years, I never met a woman on the road whom I truly liked. It was just sex. It was empty and meaningless. Detached and lonely. There was no conversation and zero connection. I was cold, like an animal.

I once heard a saying that has always stuck with me: "You're free to surrender to what you choose, but you're not free of the consequences of that choice." From the choices I was making, I risked killing myself over three minutes of fulfilling my animalistic urge—which is what sex on the road truly was to me. It meant nothing. That was all I knew, all I was capable of, and all I wanted.

Maybe the reason I couldn't love was because I didn't love myself. I thought I did, but I didn't. The Bible says to love your neighbor as yourself. If you don't love yourself, then you're not going to love your neighbor, right? Romans 13:8–10 is one of my favorite passages in the Bible. It says, "Owe nothing to anyone except for your obligation to love one another. If you love your neighbor, you will fulfill the requirement of God's law, for the commandments say you must not commit adultery; you must not murder; you must not steal; you must not covet. These and other such commandments are summed up in this one commandment: Love your neighbor as yourself. Love does no wrong to others, so love fulfills the requirement of God's law."

It's so simple. It's such a logical recipe for life. I wouldn't grasp this concept for a few years to come, but it sure makes sense. Lucky for me, there was a girl who would ultimately help me realize this.

CHAPTER 5

BLIND

When I wasn't touring, I spent most of my time working with other artists, writing my own music, and hanging around Orange County. One of my favorite places to go for sushi and cocktails was called the Drink, which after dinner hours became a club. I was pretty tight with the owner who always let me eat and drink for free. One afternoon my sister Mandi and I decided to stop in for a quick bite to eat. I was starving.

When I walked into the restaurant, I noticed three pretty young ladies sitting at the sushi bar, so I asked to be seated nearby.

I ordered some edamame, leaned over to one of the girls, and asked, "Have you ever tried this before?"

"No," she shot back, all snotty.

"It tastes like a buttery steak. You've got to try it." I thought I was being smooth and charming. And it was clear she didn't know who I was, which I liked. I finally convinced her to try one and before we knew it, we were engaged in some casual

The cover of *Fieldy's Dreams*.

conversation. She told me her name was Dena. She was a very petite girl who was wearing perfectly tight boot-cut jeans, tight white T-shirt, and all white Adidas sneakers. Even though she wasn't especially ethnic looking, I could tell she was Mexican by the way she was dressed, like a hoochie mama or "hina," which is how the Mexicans refer to women like her. I thought she was very attractive. She had hazel eyes and really full-looking, beautiful long light-brown straight hair with blond highlights like cool 1980s rocker hair. Even though I thought she looked like she might still be in high school (and she was), I thought she was really cute, so I told her I was having a party up at my house later that night and said she should come. She blew me off, saying she had plans. I shrugged it off thinking I'd never see her again.

Later that night, Dena did show up to my house, but it wasn't planned. Coincidentally, her cousin Christina had been invited to the party by some other friends. She'd called Dena around two in the morning to say she was too drunk to drive and needed her to come pick her up.

We talked for a bit. Dena said she had just turned eighteen, which was a relief. I was thirty-two years old and she looked young—very young—so I didn't want to overstep a boundary. We lived in very different worlds, but I soon learned that we came from similar backgrounds. She told me she lived with her mom and was still finishing high school. Her parents had a pretty unhealthy relationship before they got divorced. She was the same age I was when I left home. I could relate to her in a way I had never really connected with a woman before. As we got to know each other, I knew I wanted to date this girl. I asked for her phone number and invited her to come back and see me. I explained that I liked to chill at home and thought she might like to come over. I always had a lot of people around so I assured her she didn't have to worry about being alone with me.

The second time Dena came to my house, she told me she parked down the street and just sat in her car for an hour because she was so nervous. Her stomach was all knotted up and she thought she might throw up from the stress. She finally worked up the courage to come up to the house. And man, am I glad she did. From the first moment I opened the door and saw her standing there, I was convinced she was different from any other girl I'd ever met. Her soul and spirit were so full of life. I needed some of that because I was in such a dark place. She made me laugh all the time. It felt good to be around her.

When Dena and I went on our first real date, I rolled up to her mom's house to pick her up in my super-tricked-out customized Suburban. It was layered in thirty coats of silver metallic paint that sparkled and changed hues in the sunlight. The windows were tinted, and it had twenty-four-inch rims and a custom grill. The interior had fifteen different switches that controlled the air bags so I could lower the back and front, each side of the vehicle, or make it lie down like a pancake. Dena and her mother were already standing outside when I got there so I hit one of the buttons that made the truck drop to the ground, which makes a really loud and dramatic "swish" noise. I wanted to make a memorable impression. They both started laughing. In retrospect, I suppose it was kind of a macho thing to do.

Dena is really ladylike, but she's also like being with one of the dudes. She was easy to be with, could hang out with my friends, never made me feel judged, and helped me start to see things in a whole new way. She has compassion and understanding in everything she sees—in people, circumstances, and different situations.

My tricked out Suburban.

She was reluctant to date me at first. I wasn't the typical guy she was attracted to. I was thirty pounds overweight with long hair, but she was candid in telling me she liked hanging out with a rock star. She liked the carefree party lifestyle. We were just having fun with no expectations. I knew she blew me off from time to time, but I didn't care. There were lots of other women I could spend time with and that seemed okay for both of us. We liked hanging out with each other. There was no pressure for our relationship to be anything more than it was.

Dating Dena was easy. It was like having a girlfriend back in high school. Okay, she *was* in high school, but she seemed so much older to me. She was mature for her age and fun to be around. I liked her wit and sense of humor and that she was so full of life. That's hard to find in any girl—regardless of her age. The age difference hit me for the first time when Dena jokingly asked me if I wanted to go to her prom. I thought it would be fun and I knew it meant a lot to her, so I said yes. But it turned out I couldn't go. We were shooting a music video that day and it went much longer than expected. Dena was pretty cool about my not being there. She isn't the type of girl who gets mad about that kind of stuff. She understood that I had commitments. Later she told me I was too old to go, anyway. Her school had an age limit of twenty-five for prom dates.

She took a lot of razzing from the other kids at school about dating me. I'd sometimes let her drive my cars to school. She'd come rolling up in an Escalade or Benz and had to park in the teachers' lot for fear that someone might vandalize the car. Even though she was popular, she never

Celebrating
New Year's Eve
with Dena.

got caught up in the catty gossip. She could care less about what other people thought of her. I loved that because it reminded me of myself.

In my mind, she was becoming my girlfriend, but we never really talked about it. I was on the road so much that our relationship couldn't grow and thrive like a normal one. I'd be home for a minute and then gone for several months. We talked on the phone all the time. And even though I thought of her as my girlfriend, I was still out doing what I always did—drinking, taking drugs, and throwing parties on the road.

I totally believe women know when you've been a dirty dog. I think Dena always knew the truth, but she could never prove a thing, so I didn't care about getting caught. Whenever she'd ask me about other women, I'd always deny it. These were my "rules":

If your woman asks about another woman, just say "it wasn't me."

If she holds up a photo from a magazine, tell her "it isn't me."

If she presents you with copies of credit card bills, tell her "they're bogus charges." Whatever you do, use those three famous little words—deny, deny, deny.

I always knew there was no way Dena would ever find out the truth unless I someday told her. At the time, my attitude was "if you don't like it, you can leave." It would take me years to discover that getting caught wasn't what I was running from. My conscience never let me get away with a thing and there's no hiding from your own thoughts. They follow you like a loyal puppy.

Even if Dena never discovered the truth, I knew it. You will always be in turmoil when you're living a life that your inner spirit doesn't agree with. I was living in a world that was all wrapped up in me, me, wonderful me. There's not a lot of room for someone else when you believe it's all about you.

When we first met, Dena was dating a guy who was really controlling her. One night he got aggressive, and things got really physical. I was on tour in South America when she told me what happened. I couldn't handle the idea of someone hurting her, especially while I was so far away and couldn't protect her myself. So, shortly after she graduated from high school, I immediately asked her to move in with me. Somehow I believed she'd be safer living in my home than on her own.

I became fiercely protective of Dena—which essentially translated into being very controlling. If she told me she'd be home at five o'clock, she'd better be there at five sharp. I think Dena liked it because she hadn't had much of a relationship with her dad. He had been in prison for most of her life. I think we both fulfilled each other's needs. Mine was to control and hers was to feel safe.

Around eight months into dating, I finally told Dena that I loved her. We had hinted around at it before, saying silly stuff like, "I really, really like you" but I hadn't offered up the real "L" word. When I finally said those three little words, she said them right back. We were like two puppies in love.

Love is a powerful thing. People use the word *love* carelessly to describe many different types of things. You can love a Big Mac; you can love a movie; and you can love your wife. Any way you look at it, they're not all the same.

Even though I said I loved her, at the time, I had no idea what that really meant. I had never been in love. There's a passage in the Bible that I refer to all the time when I talk to people about love: 1 Corinthians 13:4–7 says, "Love is patient and kind. Love is not jealous or boastful or proud or rude. It does not demand its own way. It is not irritable and it keeps no record of being wronged. It does not rejoice about injustice, but rejoices whenever the truth wins out. Love never gives up, never loses faith, is always hopeful and endures through every circumstance."

So, looking back on the early days of my relationship with Dena, I can honestly say "I love you" meant something different to me then than it does now. We loved each other, but I was still out being a pig, fooling around and treating Dena with disrespect. I could get extremely violent if I thought she was doing something wrong. I was as abusive with my words as I was with my fists. Although I never hit her with an open hand, there was an awful lot of pushing and shoving that usually led to something more like choking.

When we partied together, we fought. We must have broken up a thousand times over the years we dated. During one particularly bad fight, I finally got Dena to admit that she was doing speed, a drug I had grown to dislike and immensely disapprove of. There was a time where I liked the up feeling I got from taking uppers, but I couldn't concentrate or focus on anything when I was taking them. I thought I was fine when I took the drug, but in reality, I'd start a bunch of little projects that I would never finish. If you've ever been to a real tweaker's house, you'll find that they've probably got a car that's half disassembled in the garage, a broken refrigerator they've probably tried to repair themselves, and half a dozen other unfinished projects. In addition, sleeping was impossible when I took speed. I like to fall asleep quickly, but when I was high on speed, my mind raced with random thoughts that usually brought on so much anxiety and stress that I couldn't shut off my mind. I started taking

(© Sebastien Paquet)

Trying to throw up a
portrait photo peace
sign at an early age.

With Mom.

Creating Korn songs for *Follow the Leader* in front of an abstract background, 1998.

Me, Head, and Munky—our first photo shoot for Ibanez Guitars.

(Reginald Arvizu Personal Archives)

Rehearsing with
L.A.P.D. in 1989.

One of my best days was
when I bought my custom
bike, but an even better
day was when I sold it. Too
dangerous for me.

I found this display while
touring in Europe. The store
was closed when I asked to
take the picture. They finally
believed it was me on the wall
and let me in to get this shot.

(Reginald Arvizu Personal Archives)

Hanging with guys from 10 Years, Stone Sour, and Avenged Sevenfold.

About to grab the camera from the photographer's hands.

Jon was helping me out with iTunes. He's a computer geek.

(Reginald Arvizu Personal Archives)

Playing a show at the
Hollywood Forever
Cemetery, June 2006.
(© Kelly Swift)

Video shoot for "Twisted Transistor" with (L-R) Jonathan,
David, Munky, David Banner, Lil Jon, Snoop Dogg, and Xzibit.

Munky and me
giving the "oh,
gee" rocker pose.

Korn performing in the
studio on the *Howard
Stern Show.*

My trademark pose.

Are you ready?

(Reginald Arvizu Personal Archives)

(©Sebastien Paquet)

My house is like a Korn museum. I have everything Korn ever did or put its name
on. These are different pieces I found in magazines from around the world.

(© Sébastien Paquet)

That's the first TRL retirement home plaque MTV gave out after they stopped playing our "Got the Life" video.
(© Sébastien Paquet)

Backstage at a show Korn played in
Europe with Tony Iommi and Geezer
Butler from Black Sabbath, 2008.
(Reginald Arvizu Personal Archives)

With Aaron from Staind and
Lajon from Sevendust.
(© Sébastien Paquet)

Getting tattooed while touring. I often
bring my tattooist with me and put him
to work! *(© Sébastien Paquet)*

On a donkey in Israel, 2005.
(Reginald Arvizu Personal Archives)

(© Sébastien Paquet)

Happy Holidays 2007 from Sarina, Dena, Israel, Fieldy, and Olivia.
(Reginald Arvizu Personal Archives)

With Israel.

Sarina and Olivia.

(Reginald Arvizu Personal Archives)

(© Sébastien Paquet)

downers to help me fall asleep, which quickly replaced the anxiety-filled angst I felt from taking speed. I took anything I could get my hands on, including Xanax, Valium, and Kolonopin, and washed them down with plenty of beer so that by the time I crawled into bed, I was so "down" I would quickly pass out. Even though I was drugged, I had the worst restless night's sleep when I was like that. I'd wake up exhausted from tossing and turning all night. It was a good plan in theory, but not very effective.

Anyway, I was afraid that Dena would end up like that, too. She had been denying her addiction for months. I assured her she could tell me the truth, saying we didn't need to hide anything from each other. I promised I wouldn't get mad.

"You can trust me," I said. "I don't care, just tell me the truth." After all, I drank and took pills every day. Of course, I had a real double standard when it came to her drug use, especially because her drug of choice was one I had come to hate.

I finally got Dena to a place where she felt vulnerable enough to confess. "Okay. I'm doing speed."

I didn't expect to but I completely freaked out. My reaction was from the gut and totally against how I really felt about Dena. I loved her but I couldn't stand the idea of being with someone who was addicted to speed.

"Get out of my house," I yelled.

I wasn't kidding. I kicked her out. I know it wasn't a fair thing to do but my history was to ruin every relationship I was in. I didn't want to get my heart broken. I know it was weak, but it was also self-protective.

Something about that particular breakup was different. Dena went back to her mom's, while I took off to New York to attend the Grammy Awards. I didn't plan to go, but breaking up with her gave me a perfect excuse to party and carouse. The funny thing was, I didn't want to.

On the flight east, I realized I was really hurting from the breakup. It felt like I had a constant pain in my heart. I had broken up with Dena and countless other women in the past and never felt like this. I checked into my hotel room and didn't want to leave. I was depressed and sad—so much so, I actually wrote a song about being heartbroken. It's the saddest, darkest song I ever wrote. My father and I later recorded it together at my home studio. It sounds like a heavy metal country song.

I ended up attending the Grammy show but felt horrible the whole night. When I got back to the West Coast, I called Dena and told her I wanted her back. I cared about this girl and didn't really want to lose her. That was the first time in our relationship where we really worked through a hard time. The relationship had shifted into something I had never had in my life. I was definitely in love.

There was so much anger, pain, and darkness trapped inside me back then. I needed to find a healthier outlet for all of those emotions. I tried to capture what was going on daily inside my head by putting those thoughts into music and releasing my first solo album, *Fieldy's Dreams,* in January 2002.

Doing my first solo album was significantly different from recording with the group. I could do whatever I wanted without answering to anyone. For example, I always felt as though my interest in rap was not being incorporated enough into the music we recorded as Korn, so during my downtime in between albums, I wrote and recorded my own songs dedicated solely to my love of hip-hop and rap. Whenever I could, I experimented with playing guitar and drums while creating a sound that was totally different from Korn. Although I was a little scared about branching out on my own, I took that fear and allowed it to motivate me to push forward instead of holding back.

It was strange not to have Jon's or Munky's opinion along the way because I've always had an appreciation for their insight and perspective when it comes to music. Working solo forced me to dig for my own opinion. It was hard at first, but I eventually came around to finding a sound I felt good about. While I did some of the beats myself, I asked up-and-coming producer Polar Bear to give me a hand. There were seventeen tracks of extremely personal and emotional tunes.

In a way, there's a goofiness to the album, which also reflected a big part of who I was and where I was at. To be completely honest, I look back on some of the songs and feel a little embarrassed about it today, but at the time, it was truly authentic material. Man, that's hard to admit, but it's true, so I have to own it.

Fieldy's Dreams didn't do that well commercially, but it was extremely important for me to purge how I was feeling. I really didn't care what anybody else thought of the work. I put together my own album, done my way with the help of some good friends, including Jonathan Davis, RBX, Son Doobie of Funkdoobiest, Tre from the Pharcyde, and Cheech Marin, and gave the world a glimpse inside my head.

One song I came up with was based on an idea I had to write a song about my love of smoking weed. I called my anthem "Are You Talkin' to Me?" The song was a really honest hard look at my addictions. Polar Bear knew this female rapper named Helluva who sang on the track with me. I was rapping to her like she was weed. When she sang back, she was answering me. Here's some of that song:

Alone at home, laying in my bed
Hearing voices in my head, leave me alone
I can't cope with the pain
Helluva:
Do you feel insane, Do you crave for cocaine?
Nope, there's other dope, Xanax,
Valium, Vicadin, and Speed
I'd rather smoke weed
Helluva:
I'm the best in the west, no stress,
sticks, stills, seeds
Fulfilling my needs, Fieldy's dreams
Searching for some weed
Ain't never gunna stop (never gunna stop),
till the day that I drop

When I played "Are You Talking to Me?" to my manager
Jeff, he freaked out. He loved it and thought it was going to
be a smash hit. He was able to get my record label to give me
a budget to film a music video down in Miami. The concept
was to have Helluva dressed up in a green fairy outfit made
out of marijuana leaves. I was dressed as a giant weed pipe
that kept circling around Helluva. It was a really cool concept
piece.

Another song on that album, "Just for Now," was something really deep for me. It was all about life—or the life I
dreamed of someday having. It was a really hard song for me
to write because it became so significant. All of the comedy
songs on the album were easy to get out. But when I wrote
this song, I felt stuck. Of course, now I know it was so challenging because I wasn't where I needed to be in my own life.
The song was authentic in words but not in my actions. It

took me close to a year to dig it out of the deepest part of my soul. The first time Jonathan sang it, the song was completely dope. It was amazing and exactly what I was looking for.

> This pain and misfortune is pure f—ing hell
> take it away nothing will change
> I will still feel the same this is too much pain
> Am I being tortured time will only tell
> Am I insane (nyaah) or am I in hell
> Gotta have faith (nyaah) not someone to
> escort you (nyaah . . . nyaah)
> Live your own life no reason to rebel (nyaah)
> All of this hatred this has to be hell

One final song on the album I am especially proud of is "Ortiz Anthem," a song I wrote to honor my good friend Tito Ortiz. We knew each other back in the day while I was living in Huntington Beach. He'd become a famous ultimate fighter. His spirit and tenacity inspired me to write the song. When I played it for him in my car, he was speechless.

Here's a couple of verses:

> Bow down to me you sissy la la,
> I'm gunna bounce on your face,
> like 64 impala, when you see me in the ring,
> and I pop my collar, remember whose a king,
> Ortiz, a pimp balla, adrenalin rush,
> enough to throw a truck,
> before I put you in this pain, I wish
> you a lot of luck,
> If you didn't know I was insane,
> and I don't give'a f— buck buck,

Tito's in the ring, scream,
Ortiz please the crowd , bow to your knees,
Tito's in the ring, scream,
knock you out without a doubt,
it's good to be the king,
Tito's in the ring, scream,
scream and shout, gunna knock this fool out,
Tito's in the ring, scream,
Ortiz please the crowd, bow to your knees

With Tito Ortiz and Jon.

A lot of people were surprised by my attraction to hip-hop, rappers, and street style. All the guys in Korn used to endlessly harass me about it, saying I was a wannabe rapper. I was trying hard to live the gangsta lifestyle—big house, lots of cars, and lots of bling. I don't know why, but I've always related to those guys in a way I never did metal dudes.

I used to hang out with Tre from the Pharcyde. We were good friends for a long time. He ended up doing "Who Got the Dough," with me for *Fieldy's Dreams*. We were tight, often sitting around, talking for hours. When we wrote "Who Got the Dough" together, I asked Tre if he'd rap what I wrote. And then I suggested he write a verse that I would rap. I told him to write whatever was in his heart and I'd do the same. We went into the studio and recorded each other's rhymes. We've lost contact over the years, but he was a cool dude to hang with.

I also hung out with Bubba Sparxxx a lot. I did a music video with him playing bass with Travis Barker on the drums. I also did a song with legendary rapper E-40. I was a big fan so when I heard he was up in Oakland recording, I told him I'd come to him if he was interested in working together. He said he'd send his limo to pick me up from the airport. The car that arrived was a white 1970s limousine with a red velvet roof. The window tint was so dulled it looked almost purple. The interior was the original leather, but completely worn out. That car was completely ghetto.

Much to my surprise, E-40's house was spectacular. I'm not sure what I expected, but this pad was a showplace. It was all white on the inside. All of the furniture and interior features were pristine. He told me I had to take my shoes off before I could enter. There was a line of everyone's shoes by the front door, which I thought was kind of funny. It wasn't the image I had of E-40.

We hung out all night, recording a track I played bass on in his home studio. I'm not sure he ever used the song for anything but I was happy to get to know the guy. He called me a few months later to see if I wanted to be in a music video he was doing with another rapper named Fabolous, who has since become famous. I immediately said yes and flew back up to Oakland.

They shot the video in an old apartment building in the projects. My "big" part was answering the door in a scene where I was dressed in goggles wearing an apron and no shirt underneath. My hair was soaking wet, which made me completely unrecognizable. E-40 played my landlord who was looking for my rent. When I answered the door, I was holding a big wad of cash that I ended up throwing in his face.

I like being in music videos, but I really have no desire to act. I love playing music and doing my thing. The closest I ever came to acting in the early days was when Korn did an episode of *South Park* in 1999.

And then there was that one lost episode of MTV's *Punk'd*. The band was in the studio in 2004 working on our *Greatest Hits* album. We were working at Jon's home studio redoing a couple of songs. Everybody was in on the plan, except, of course, me.

The original idea was to have me come home from our last tour to a prop plane that looked like it crashed into the top of my house. For whatever reasons—I think it was a 9/11 thing—that plan didn't work out.

I was later told another concept was to have Dena's family from Mexico living in my home while we were out touring. That one didn't work out, either. The final plan was ultimately put into place.

Here's what happened.

I drove up to Jon's studio as usual. It was a clear, perfect

blue-sky California day. I sat in the lounge for a few minutes talking to the guys when I noticed white smoke coming
out of the ceiling. Even though I saw it, no one else seemed
concerned so I didn't say anything. Finally, the smoke got so
thick and low it became alarming.

Jon screamed, "Fire! We've got to get out of here!"

Everyone in the studio was freaking out. The guys ran out
of the studio acting scared and panicked. Something inside
told me what was up, so I casually walked outside and said,
"We're getting Punk'd."

No one caved. They kept right on scrambling around talking about how to get our equipment out and whether anyone
called the fire department. By the time I got around the corner
of the studio, there was a fire truck at the end of Jon's driveway trying to get past his big iron gate. Firemen came walking
up the driveway in full gear, shields over their faces, ready
to go to work. It was so hot out, I could see them sweating
through their face masks. I kept insisting this was a prank,
but no one gave in.

"We got a call about smoke?" A very official looking fireman started talking to Jon. He went on to say that the smoke
was very toxic and if anyone had breathed it in we could die.
The fireman said there had been several similar instances in the
neighborhood that made this fire cause for concern. He told
us all to sit over on the ledge of the wall that surrounded Jon's
driveway.

"I'm not sitting down over there," I protested. "You can't tell
me what to do." Instead, I walked over and sat on one of Jon's
three-wheelers on the opposite side of the driveway. I looked over
and noticed a Suburban in the driveway with blacked-out windows. I automatically assumed there were cameramen inside.

The fireman kept asking if any of us breathed in the smoke.

Finally, I jumped up and asked to see some identification. I wanted these jokers to show me they were really firemen. When I approached one of the guys, he somehow managed to pull my shirt off. I don't know how he did it—maybe he used to be a stripper or something but he was far too good at getting my shirt off in one pull. I stood stunned and shirtless in Jon's driveway.

"We'll need your shirt for sampling at the lab." That's what the fireman said.

"Whatever." Now I was pissed off.

"Man, you have a sucky job. Look at you sweating in there!" It was like I was taunting that cop back in Denver all over again. You would have thought I learned a valuable lesson from mouthing off to that cop. I didn't care. I was absolutely certain this was all a big hoax.

"I need to get my cell phone. It's inside the studio." I was insistent.

I threatened to go into the studio if someone didn't go get my phone. The fireman took off his mask, looked me in the eyes, and said he'd go in and get it. When he came out, it occurred to me that *if* there was really toxic smoke, he was now exposed, too. When I called him out, he told me not to worry about him.

Just then, I noticed a couple of other firemen pulling a large, plastic, square, bubble-looking thing up the driveway that said *Biohazard* on the sides. Two black gloves were attached to the plastic cube that someone could put their hands into so they didn't have to touch whatever was inside. Behind them, a couple more guys were pulling a black tank with a hose attached to it.

The fireman looked at me and said, "You've got to strip down and get in there. We need to squirt you with these chemicals to decontaminate you. If we don't, your skin could burn right off." There was no way I was getting inside that bubble. Jon kept saying we should get inside to make sure we were okay.

"You go first," I said.

Since he was in on the joke, he played along. Jon stripped down to his underwear, stood inside the bubble, and let these guys hose him down thinking I'd go next. The joke was on him because that was never going to happen. I decided to taunt the fireman some more.

I walked over to the pool and said, "Hey, watch this. I'm going to stick my arm in the pool to see if my skin melts off."

"No! Stop!" The fireman tried to stop me but I dunked my arm in the pool anyway.

"Hey, look at this. My skin isn't melting off."

I walked back over to see Jon in the bubble just as they turned on the hose. He screamed as loud as he could—and if you've ever been to a Korn show, you know Jon can let loose. It turned out the water was ice cold. That was part of the punk. They wanted to squirt me down with freezing water. I was done playing along. I turned around and headed for the studio. When I opened the door, a bunch of cameramen and crew guys were sitting around.

I looked back at the fireman and said, "You can't punk a dog!" and started barking at them. Everyone was laughing. Later I found out there were cameras hidden everywhere. Even though I thought they did a really good job, I refused to sign any of the releases—I didn't want to look like a fool. They wanted to make it look like they got me, but I wouldn't budge and I told them I'd only agree if they used the footage as it happened. They wouldn't do it, so that episode never aired. Hey, Ashton, if for some reason you're reading this— better luck next time!

COMING UNDONE

y early 2002, the band was deep into writing the *Untouchables* album. It had been three years since our last album, *Issues,* had been released, which meant a lot of time had passed since all of us had been in the studio together. Tensions had been growing between the members of the band. For the most part, I wasn't getting along with David at all. Although my relationship with Munky was pretty strained, too, I had gotten to a place where I totally closed myself off to David, though we were always cordial. I could be nice without having to ask the guy to dinner. It had been like that for years.

Looking back, I think the guys had gotten pretty fed up with me and my behavior. My partying wasn't the biggest problem because all of us were pretty much riding the same train, except Jon who had gotten sober in 2000. I think we were all getting sick of one another, especially after a long night of partying. There's a certain part of those nights where

In the studio rockin' out.

seemingly normal people will turn into some crazy alternative version of themselves, especially when there's drinking and drugs involved. People would literally hide from me if I had been at it all night. "Oh no . . . here comes Fieldy." I could hear people saying those exact words even if I wasn't aware of what they really meant. Before he got sober, there were plenty of times I used to hide from Jonathan for fear he had turned into Jack O'clock, the aggressive Jon I mentioned earlier. He'd walk onto my bus and I'd pretend to be asleep, afraid that he might be just wasted enough to do something crazy, like bite me, which he had done in the past.

When Jon partied, he had a passion for starting arguments about anything just to start a fight. When Munky got wasted, I'd refer to him as "drunken Munky." We all just learned to stay away from one another when we were high. I think knowing that made it easier to avoid potentially explosive confrontations.

Admittedly, I was probably the biggest bully of the bunch. When I was drunk, I had no filter whatsoever, so anything could fly out of my mouth without a warning. People eventually learned to laugh at me, tune whatever I said out, and just walk away. Even so, I am sure they were never able to forget some of the cruel comments I made.

We had gotten to the point where the guys were happy to play together but none of us wanted to hang out. I think the only reason I was allowed to stay in the band was because they liked my bass playing, unique style, input, and ideas. I should have been kicked out numerous times. But I wasn't. If someone else was acting the way I was back then, I would have lobbied hard to push that person out.

The guys must have figured out that they couldn't change me. It was a lot easier to find a way to work around all of the obstacles my behavior put in our way than it was to expect me to change. So they adapted to keep the group together. The truth is, people won't usually change for anyone else. They have to do it for themselves. I wasn't ready to transform my life yet nor did I know that there was a need to.

In an effort to bring some sense of solidarity back to the group, we decided to set up in Scottsdale, Arizona, for a few months. We thought the new environment would help inspire us to write all the songs for our new album.

The five of us rented four separate houses, which was a condition of working together. Besides, all of us were pretty much partying like rock stars at the time and needed our space. Munky and Head ended up sharing theirs while David, Jon, and I each had our own pad. It cost around ten thousand dollars a month for each home but it was worth it—there was no way we could have all lived and worked together. The amount of money we spent making that album was ridiculous, but we didn't care because in our minds, it wasn't our money (although, of course, it was). The record company was handling all the bills, so we all acted like spending hundreds of thousands of dollars was no big deal.

As I mentioned, even though I cared a lot about Dena, I still hadn't given up my adulterous ways on the road. Scottsdale was probably the worst betrayal of trust because I told her we were there to work. I had girls coming and going all the time. I'd fly chicks in from wherever, have my personal assistant Ham pick them up at the airport in one of my nice cars, hang with them for a day or two, and then send them on their way.

Let me tell you a little bit about Ham. He wasn't just my assistant—he was one of my good friends. I first met him through Munky in Bakersfield. He spent a lot of time touring with the band over the years. We all thought he was a cool dude. I'm not sure what happened, but Ham and Munky had some type of falling-out. I liked the guy a lot and was looking for someone to help me out so I hired him.

I was partying so hard, I couldn't even take care of the simple stuff in life like making sure I could get back and forth to the studio on time. I was usually too wasted to drive, so Ham drove me to the studio, when we went out just to hang, to appearances, pretty much everywhere I needed to go. When the driving was done, he and I usually partied together, at the end of the night. That's how we became such good friends. We spent a lot of time together which gave us huge windows of opportunity to talk, so he knew everything about my life and I about his.

Ham always had my back. We sounded a lot alike, so he'd pretend to be me. He used to call my mom for me because I was too high to talk to her myself. He even called Dena a few times so she'd think I was checking in. At the time, I didn't think it wast freaky or weird. He was saving me from the embarrassment of not being able to talk to the most important people in my life. That's how pathetic things had gotten.

Ham often covered my tracks by making amends on my behalf. I'd mouth off to people all the time, and afterward, Ham would apologize for me, explaining I was too intoxicated to know what I was doing. He was my "fix it" guy. Every drunk needs someone to patch up the debris of destruction they leave behind. I'd wake up in the morning unable to remember a thing from the night before. I didn't know who I saw, spoke to, how I got home, nothing. Ham was my eyes, my ears, and, since I didn't have one, my conscience.

Sometimes, after he'd drop me off at night, I'd wander the hallways of whatever hotel we were at, bleary-eyed and wasted, looking for food. I'd take the leftovers off other people's room service trays that had been left outside their doors. There were some nights I'd search five or six floors, only to come up empty-handed. Other nights I scored, scamming half-eaten burgers or leftover fries without a care in the world as to whose mouths had been all over that food before me.

All of that drunken late-night binge eating was really getting to me. I was pushing close to two hundred pounds on the scales, which is thirty to forty pounds more than my frame can hold. Booze and food had always been a wicked combination.

Writing in Arizona was one big party. When we were done creating the music, I made it a point to go out and blow off some steam. When the bars and clubs closed, I came back to the house to party some more. My house was by far the biggest party palace of the four. (To be fair, David's was a close second.) I even had a stripper pole installed for "entertainment." And when I didn't have the strippers come to me, I went to them.

While we were working I heard Pantera was playing in Phoenix. Vinnie Paul, Dimebag Darrell, and me hung out a lot back in the day. They had a tanning bed at their place in Texas that I used from time to time whenever I was in town. I'd go over to tan and ended up jamming with those guys for hours. I'm pretty sure we recorded some of our stuff over the years, but I've never heard it. Man, I can't even imagine the sound of it today. Vinnie was on the drums, Dimebag played guitar, and I hit the bass. We could jam all night when we got together. Those were good times, for sure.

Anyway, Vinnie called to say they were in Phoenix doing a gig. We made a plan to go out after the show. Ham, my buddy Jamie, and RBX (Snoop Dogg's cousin), Vinnie, and

Partying with Vinnie Paul from Pantera.

me wound up at a local strip club. I was never terribly comfortable in strip clubs. They were just an easy place to go in whatever city we were in. Even so, I had spent a lot of time at this particular club while working in Scottsdale so I was well acquainted with all the girls. I knew Vinnie would dig hanging out there, so after their show, we headed straight to the club.

I was drunk before we got there, and as the night went on, I got totally trashed.

At one point, I mumbled and slurred, "I'm sick of this place. I want to leave."

For some reason, I was anxious to get out of there. I stood up to leave. I didn't care who was coming with me. I was out of there. Ham looked around for Vinnie, but he was nowhere to be found. I wasn't waiting around. Even though Vinnie was a good friend, I was too wasted to reason with so we left. As we were pulling out of the parking lot, I caught a glimpse of Vinnie coming out of the club. I laughed as I told the driver to keep going. The next time I saw Vinnie, he was cool about the whole thing. We partied hard together over the years, so he knew the score.

I shared my house in Scottsdale with my buddy and bodyguard Loc. He worked security with Korn from the very beginning. Prior to starting with us, Loc worked for the New Kids on the Block and Michael Jordan.

Loc was no joke. He took his job protecting the band very seriously. When we first met him, Loc showed up wearing a suit and tie, like he was straight from the Secret Service. He'd even run alongside our limo until we got rolling and would jump in the front seat with the driver just before we sped off. We'd all laugh at him because we never really thought we needed such a serious guy working security. Eventually we told Loc we wanted him to ride in the back with us. He was reluctant until we threatened to fire him if he didn't.

Once we all got to know him, we tried to get Loc to loosen up. I told him he didn't have to wear his suit and tie. In fact, it made me feel uncomfortable. Loc and I began to get to know each other one-on-one, and before too long, he became my personal security guy. Head and Jonathan ended up hiring Josh, a friend of mine who used to date my sister Mandi, to look after them. He was a big dude with a shaved head. Even though he didn't have any official training, you wouldn't want to meet up with him in a dark alley. Josh and I were really tight until he could no longer take my loose mouth. I said a lot of hurtful and negative things and eventually pushed him away as a friend.

When we got to Scottsdale, one of the most important things I asked Loc to do for me was to make sure I always had clean sheets on my bed. Even though changing my linens was not his job, Loc seemed cool doing it so I never gave my request a second thought.

One night, I came home completely wasted from the clubs to discover there were no sheets on my bed. I freaked out. I started screaming and yelling like a madman. I walked into Loc's room to confront him, but he wasn't there. I flew into an uncontrollable rage, picking up his bed and tossing it over. I grabbed his dressers and threw them across the room. I smashed his lamp onto the floor, swinging it like I was Pete Townsend smashing a guitar. I picked up his laptop and threw it as hard as I could, smashing it into a thousand little pieces. I ripped the whole room apart. It was trashed so bad it looked like a tornado had come through.

Before I could finish my trail of destruction, Josh came up from behind me, put me in a choke hold, and dragged me out of there. I was still trying to wreck everything in sight as he pulled me across the floor. When Loc got home, he was speechless when he saw what I had done. He left the house without saying a word. I think he spent the night at Jon's house. His silence sobered me up pretty fast.

The next day, I tried to apologize, offering to pay for all of the damages. I felt bad but all the money in the world wasn't going to fix the harm I had done to our relationship. My longtime friendship with Loc was ruined beyond repair. He stayed with the band, but refused to work with me.

Once my friendship with Loc was over, I started hanging out with this dude I called "Care Bear," who worked as the engineer on *Fieldy's Dreams*. In retrospect, I'm surprised he wanted to have anything to do with me because I had been pretty cruel to him in the past. I once hit him with my bass guitar because my pedal wasn't working or some dumb reason like that. I whacked him as hard as I could, swinging my bass like a Louisville Slugger. He had a huge bruise on his arm for weeks. I fired him, but somehow managed to stay friends.

At the time, I didn't realize what a jerk I was. I thought I could get away with trashing other people's stuff because I could afford to pay for the damages. I treated people so bad, especially people who worked for me, like Care Bear or Loc. These guys were my friends. They didn't deserve my wrath—not for any price. I can't imagine doing anything like that sober, but back then, it happened more than I'd like to admit because I was always whacked out of my mind.

Even though Shela and I were divorced, I couldn't stop thinking about the peace she seemed to have with her new-found faith. I started to become interested in some of the facets of her beliefs as a Jehovah's Witness because she was raising our daughters to believe in those teachings. My buddy Jamie had a daughter who was also being raised the same way so he and I would often talk about some of the aspects of that religion we could both embrace. I liked that it wasn't a flashy religion. People didn't wear big crosses around their necks to prove their love for God. It seemed like everyone was equal, which I totally respected. And though I never came around to accepting those ideas for myself, it got me thinking about a belief in a higher power and, for the first time in my life, something much bigger than myself.

We finished writing *Untouchables* and headed back to L.A. to record it. This was our fifth album, and things were getting tougher between the guys in the band. None of us wanted to hang together outside of the time we spent working in the studio. I was becoming more withdrawn. I had even begun to slowly distance myself from my parents.

Dad was now remarried to Mindi, a woman I liked but barely knew. When they got married, Dad completely turned his life around. He was now living a completely sober and Christian life. He was very committed to studying God's word and spreading His love. I didn't know much about his lifestyle, and, like Shela's newfound faith, I wanted nothing to do with it. Dad spoke to me from time to time about the teachings of Jesus but he never preached. He and his wife came to visit but it was generally superficial interaction. Even though I know he didn't agree with the way I was living my life, he never made me feel judged. All he wanted to do was to show me love.

And *that* scared me . . . a lot.

I suppose it was one of the reasons I pushed Dad away. I didn't want to get my heart broken again. The more love Dad showed, the colder I turned toward him. I didn't show him any affection or warmth.

My mother has always loved me with open arms but our relationship was never the same after she and Dad got divorced. I tried to connect with her over the years, going up to visit her in Bakersfield when I wasn't on tour. She, too, never voiced her opinion to me, but I knew she could see that my life was spinning out of control. All mothers know when their children are in trouble.

I believe all personal darkness comes from having a broken heart. I've mentioned that my first heartbreak came when Mom and Dad told me they were getting divorced. From that day on, all I wanted to do was numb myself from the constant aching pain I felt. I used alcohol, drugs, and food as my crutches. I never wanted to feel a broken heart again.

Even though I was so disrespectful to women, I pretty

much only had female friends growing up. I had very few dude friends. I used to always make girls cry. I'd do anything to make sure they couldn't hurt me first. I remember being out with a girl one night in high school, driving in my Toyota pickup truck.

I turned to her and said, "You know, I could kill us right now." She had absolutely no idea where this demonic behavior was coming from. I suddenly yanked the steering wheel hard to the right so we'd swerve off the road.

"You're scaring me." She was panicked and began to cry.

"Shut up!" I was inexplicably angry. "Do you want me to kill us right now?" I screamed as I yanked the wheel again swerving left and then right.

She was hysterical and out of control, sobbing uncontrollably out of fear and sheer panic.

Then I turned toward her and said, "I'm just kidding."

I don't know why I did stuff like that. Inside, I had to make girls cry. It was as much a need as eating or sleeping. Maybe I held on to some anger toward my mother all of these years because she represented the opposite sex—the enemy. I didn't want to let any woman get close to my heart, including my mom. Even though my relationship with Dena was the best I'd ever had, I still had no qualms about cheating on her. I used marriage as a spiteful device in the past, pretending to be a husband when I was just a pig. I was mean and thoughtless. I didn't care about the women I had married. Marrying them was like a cruel joke on them because I knew from the very beginning I didn't want to be in that type of a relationship. I was abusive in every way. I guess it's what I learned growing up.

Over the years, I learned to tune out my parents' fights. All I wanted to see were two people in love. And for years, my parents somehow seemed to make their relationship work. I grew up viewing love as emotional and sometimes violent. That's what I truly believed was normal.

That is how I loved.

Angry, numb, and with a broken heart.

I often wondered why anyone would want to stay with a guy like me. I was thirty-five pounds overweight, had big, black circles under my eyes, and looked like I was a walking dead man. I lived my life believing I could fill the black void in my heart by getting high and spending money. I'd get ripped until I just passed out only to get the worst night's sleep. I'd wake up the next day shaking and throwing up so bad I'd take a handful of pills and smoke weed to make all of my pain go away.

I was anxious all the time.

I couldn't sit still—ever.

Even when I was trying to get into a girl's pants, if she kept me waiting too long, I moved on.

Maybe I was living my life for one reason: I was trying to find love.

But I had no clue how to do it.

From the time I was a freshman in high school, I only knew how to live one way— *Fieldy's* way.

It was painfully clear *that* wasn't working; I was lonely, depressed, and spinning out of control. And though I know deep down we all loved one another, even my relationships with Head, Munky, Jon, and David were falling apart.

I've been through a lot with those guys over the years. As we became more famous and my partying got to an uncontrollable point, it seemed like none of us were really getting along. By the time we left to promote *Untouchables,* there wasn't a lot of interaction outside of playing together. Even the women in our lives couldn't see eye to eye.

Dena and Jon's wife, Deven, had some tension between them all throughout our 2002 European tour that escalated to a place I'll never understand, a place that *only* women can go to. I guess there was some altercation between them that took place before a show. Jon and I were completely oblivious to what had transpired. We did our show as usual. When I came offstage, Dena was steaming pissed. Alcohol probably played a role in her anger, but I didn't really think she was serious. Thinking she was just overreacting, I told her I'd go tell Jon that she wanted to fight his wife, thinking it would defuse the situation. Man, was I wrong.

When I walked into Jon's dressing room and told him Dena wanted to fight Deven, it triggered an unexpected crazy, insane reaction. Jon and Deven flipped out. He told me the guys had had it with me and wanted me out of the band.

I felt sick. After everything we had been through, it all came down to this? My nerves were so bad thinking I was getting kicked out of Korn.

The next night I heard that David, Munky, and Jon were having a secret, behind-closed-door meeting in Jon's hotel room to vote me out. I couldn't let them do that without putting up a fight. I knocked on the door and asked if I could come in. They refused. I couldn't believe they wouldn't face me. We had recently talked about kicking David out of the band and had the decency to talk to him face-to face. Why wouldn't they extend the same courtesy to me? I was freaking out. I kept apologizing through the door, saying I was sorry, but nothing seemed to be working. They wouldn't open the door. I humbled myself in a way I had never done before. My attitude was always so nonchalant. I was arrogant and selfish. I wasn't sure why the guys were angling to kick me out this particular time. They sure had lots of reasons to do so in the past. I thought, *This is it. I'm through.* And there was nothing I could do about it.

I sent Jon a dozen roses the following day with a note that read, "I'm sorry." He never responded. I didn't know what to expect when we played our show later that night, but it was like nothing was wrong. Afterward, we all hugged it out. It was clear that all was forgiven. I was wrong for acting like such a jerk to these guys who were my brothers. I didn't want to be kicked out of the band, so I'd refused to stand on ceremony or let my ego stand in the way of doing what was right. That wasn't my usual tack. The thought of no longer being in Korn stunned me into doing the right thing. And, to be sure, I should never have gotten involved in a rift between Dena and Deven. (Guys: Take note. It's never a good idea to get in between chick fights.)

I made a lot of bad decisions over the years. From the outside looking in, I had the life. I was a huge rock star living in a big mansion with an elevator, had the sickest rock pool I've ever seen in a home, and all of the trappings that go with that grand lifestyle. Even so, I hardly ever went home. I preferred to stay in dumpy hotels in Hollywood or crash in the studio. And when I did go to that house, I'd throw wild parties with a bunch of drugs and alcohol and let people trash the place. I'd wake up the next morning and have to pay thousands of dollars to have someone come fix everything that was damaged.

And for what?

I'll never really know.

I kept thinking about the peace Dad and Shela had in their lives and realized I didn't feel that way anywhere I went. I'd smoke a joint in one room and move on to another in an attempt to find a place where I felt comfortable, even at home. I was so uncomfortable in my own skin, and there was no possible way I could enjoy anything else because I had no serenity in my life. You can have happiness, love, and fun, but without peace, you will never enjoy the "things" you have. I should know. I tried and failed. Miserably.

As Korn's success grew, I foolishly spent thousands of dollars on ridiculous jewelry, expensive cars, private planes, trips to Vegas with friends, and of course, partying. I was living in a house with a fifteen-car garage and felt an obligation to fill each and every stall. I could spend money as fast as I drank beer. I'd impulsively buy a car, let it sit in my driveway because I was hardly ever home long enough to drive it, and turn around and sell it for a fraction of the purchase price. Or sometimes, I'd buy a car, pouring tens of thousands of dollars

This is what it looks like when I'm playing to a big outdoor crowd.

into fixing it up, and sell it for a loss. It didn't take long for all of that money to add up.

My accountant tried to tell me I was living too large, but I didn't want to hear his advice. I figured we could just get back into the studio, cut another album, go on tour, and my cash problems would disappear. I wasn't in deep debt, but I did have to take out a second mortgage to cover my overhead until I could get back on my feet.

I spent the next two years focused on recording and touring. We headlined at Ozzfest, toured Europe, recorded our sixth album, *Take a Look in the Mirror,* and put out our first *Greatest Hits* album.

It was grueling, but between the tours and records, I managed to pull myself out of debt. I don't ever want to worry about money again. The pressure was excruciating. I thank

Me and Head.

God every day Dena stood by my side throughout that struggle. If I ever worried she might have been with me for my
money, those days proved to me otherwise.

Things with the band were going well. As we started to
earn more money, our managers did everything they could
to make life on the road more comfortable for us. When we
toured for *Take a Look in the Mirror,* they offered to get each
of us our own tour buses and separate hotel rooms on the
road. They explained that the newer buses really cost the
same as the older larger ones we had been using, but each
had its own bedroom in the back and only six bunks instead
of twelve. Having my own room sounded even better than
separate buses. The separation was also a lot more convenient
when our families came on the road.

Once we were all given our own space, it was a lot easier
for us to get along. We were never forced to hang out with
anyone unless we wanted to. That tour was different from the
previous ones because I really only saw the guys in the dressing room fifteen or twenty minutes before a show or backstage
afterward. We usually had loud music blaring in the dressing
room to help get us pumped, so even if you wanted to talk
to someone, it was all but impossible because the music was
blasting. The rest of the time was primarily spent on our own,
away from one another.

Sometime during that tour, I noticed Head had stopped
coming to the dressing room. He started going from his tour
bus directly to the stage. Nobody really thought anything of
it. I don't think I ever saw him before a single show for the
next few years. I did notice that Head got really skinny. Every
time I caught a glimpse of him walking from his bus to the
stage, he always had a beer in his hand and was walking so
fast that he never made eye contact. His energy was almost

frantic. When I see one of the guys before a show, any conversation we do have is usually pretty short and almost always about getting pumped for the show. The dialogue goes something like this:

"Hey, man. You ready to rock?"

"Let's do it!"

And that's about all we say. It isn't the time to ask someone how their day is going or to make random small talk. So the lack of dialogue between Head and me wasn't that unusual. I just figured he was drinking a lot and that's why I always saw him holding a beer. Of course, I would later discover that he was drinking before every show to come down from all of the speed he was doing. (I only found this out after reading Head's book where he admitted that he spent most of his time on that tour in the back of his bus getting high on speed.)

We had become a band of brothers, and yet, there was a civil but clear separation when we were on the road. To some extent, some of us were just co-workers. I knew that David was having a lot of issues with some of my erratic behavior, but we never talked about it or argued over how he felt. We remained social, like two people who work in an office that are friendly and polite but hardly (if ever) hang out together. None of us ever wanted to be confrontational with one another. We just wanted to do our thing—play our music and live our lives in peace. And that is pretty much how the next few years went down.

That is, until February 2005, when Korn was rocked by the news that Head was leaving the band. We were in the middle of recording our eighth studio album, *See You on the Other Side,* when Head made his departure. Munky came to the studio one day and told all of us he'd received an e-mail from Head saying he was quitting. Head may have sent me an

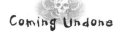

Playing a free show at a Best Buy in Hollywood to promote a new album, and one of the last appearances before Head left.

e-mail, too, but I wasn't very good at checking my inbox back then, so I don't recall ever getting it. If I did, I'm sure I never read it. Munky told us that Head was planning to come to the studio to talk to us in person, but that never happened. It was clear that he had made his final decision, and for him, there was no turning back.

Amid lots of speculation that the band was breaking up, we decided to release the following statement:

> *Korn has parted ways with guitarist Brian "Head"*
> *Welch, who has chosen Jesus Christ as his savior, and*
> *will be dedicating his musical pursuits to that end. Korn*
> *respects Brian's wishes, and hope he finds the happiness*
> *he's searching for.*

None of us wanted Head to leave the band. He did what he had to do to follow his path. I knew that Head had found spiritual enlightenment—something that felt very far away from where my thoughts and actions were at the time. I couldn't understand his need to leave the band to pursue his newfound faith. I completely respected his need to be with his young daughter who had no one else to look after her, but I was confused by his decision to leave us behind.

At the time, I acted like it was no big deal. But it shook me to the core. Not so much the act of leaving, but rather, his need to separate from his brothers. We were a family. When Head quit, I felt like I lost much more than a bandmate. The sacrifices Head was making left me feeling bewildered, which made his decision to abandon us even harder to fully embrace and support.

Even so, I knew life had to continue on. Korn wasn't going to fall apart or break up without Head. None of us were ready to quit. On the contrary, we were all eager to keep pushing forward and not let Head's departure drag us down. We chose to take a positive approach to our new dynamic.

Munky and I got back to our core writing of music together like we did in the L.A.P.D. days. We had been gunning to re-create our sound. Head's departure forced us to make some changes and welcome a new wave of creativity that now washed over the band.

We finished recording *See You on the Other Side,* which sounded really different from our previous work. All of us played harder than ever, becoming better musicians and performers in the process. In fact, when we performed, I enjoyed having the extra room on the stage. I had always been a little crowded because Head and I stood to the right side of the stage while I was stuck in between Jon and him. Now that

Head was gone, I didn't feel crammed in anymore. I'm really active onstage so it was nice to have that half of the stage to myself. Still, I missed the chemistry of having Head on-stage—he was and will always be an amazing musician and a dynamic performer. His creative guitar playing brought a different style to Korn, a sound that no one else could truly duplicate.

After Head left, we kept in touch a little, but our lives were in very different places. I went up to Bakersfield to visit him to see how he was doing. When I walked into his house, I noticed all of his plaques and gold records were ripped off the wall. He told me he had to get rid of all those things because he was moving on with his life. I was surprised but acted unfazed.

Head spoke about how great his life was, saying leaving the band was the best thing that ever happened to him. He even tried to convince me that I should join him on his walk with the Lord, saying we could start our own band and get the rest of the guys to open their eyes and change their lives, too. I didn't agree with him at all. I couldn't abandon the band. They were my friends, my family. I didn't feel like I had to leave the band to get my life together. I tried to tell Head that we were all still his friends, too, but no one was ever going to change because *he* wanted them to. If we were to change our lives, it would have to be at our own pace. If we didn't, that would have to be cool, too.

I was glad Head was no longer killing himself by doing drugs. He looked the best I'd seen him look in years. When he asked about the new album, I could tell he didn't really want me to answer. I was trying to be sensitive, but things just took a downward spiral. We got into an argument over our difference of opinion on his need to leave the band and my lack of understanding about his newfound relationship with

Jesus. At the peak of our argument, Head told me to lose his number until I got straight with God.

"I'll never be straight with God. I'm not holy. If I was, I wouldn't need Jesus as the middleman. God can't see sin. If I was straight with God, I'd be like Moses back in the day with a direct line to talk to God myself." I was so angry about the whole subject. And, looking back, a bit misinformed, too.

I looked Head square in the eyes and said, "I'm never going to call you again because I'm never going to be straight with God." And that was the last time we talked for quite some time.

Photo for the *"See You on the Other Side"* CD insert.

7

GOOD GOD

I once heard a story about a grandfather and his grandson. The grandfather was trying to explain to the young boy that we all have two dogs that live inside of us that are at war with our soul. One is good and the other bad.

"Which one will win the war, Grandpa?" the boy asked.

"Whichever one you feed," the old man answered.

I've always related to that story because I spent the first thirty-four years of my life perfecting feeding the bad dog. I lived by my own set of rules—*Fieldy's Rules*. It took me years to see that I was feeding the wrong dog.

You have a choice to live on one side or the other. There's no living in between the two. Me, I got really good at being bad, and I didn't care.

I didn't think twice about the fact that I was hurting lots of people around me or was doing ireparable damage to myself . . . that is, until I found out my father was dying from cancer.

My Dad.

I was on my way to the Korn studio where we were busy recording *See You on the Other Side* when I received a call from Dad's wife, Mindi. She said Dad had a cyst on the back of his neck that he wanted removed. It was supposed to be no big deal, but the doctors gave him an antibiotic after the surgery that he had a really bad reaction to. As a result, Dad was forced to stay in the hospital a lot longer than anyone expected. During that time, the doctors told us they believed Dad had cancer.

When Dad got sick, I thought I could fix him because I had money, power, and influence. I was rich and famous, right? I thought I could fix anything. I tried to reassure Dad that everything would be fine. I offered to send him to the best doctors and hospitals to get him well. Money was no object. But he insisted on seeing his own physician at a hospital where his insurance would cover the treatment.

All throughout his illness, I pretended that nothing bad was happening to him. I'd stop by the hospital every day for an hour or two so he didn't feel scared or alone. Seeing him there made me realize I didn't spend nearly enough time with Dad before he got sick, mostly because I was on the road a lot and, I suppose, because I was selfish back then. I spent hours in the hospital talking about all the things we could do when he got better. I thought that would inspire him to heal quicker. I wasn't ready for my dad to die.

Spending time with him was strange because he looked so fragile and weak. I wasn't used to seeing Dad look so bad. He had brown, black, and blue spots all over his arms and legs. He had what looked like track marks on his arms from all of the shots and IV needles they needed to give him. Dad was a superhero to me. I didn't think anything could ever touch him. I knew he was in pain, but I still acted as if nothing was wrong.

Even though test after test came back negative, the doctors

kept insisting Dad had cancer. I refused to believe it. There was no evidence supporting their claim. The doctors wanted to do a bone marrow test to confirm the diagnosis, explaining it would be excruciatingly painful. Even so, they were encouraging him to have the test so we could finally have some definitive answers.

The test came back negative. No cancer. Even then, the doctors vehemently continued to persist with their diagnosis. They suggested removing a lymph node from his neck to do another test. That, too, came back with no traces of cancer.

I finally got fed up with the medical care Dad was getting and insisted on moving him to another hospital. My managers helped me track down one of the top specialists in the world at Cedars-Sinai Hospital in Los Angeles. Much to my surprise, and though there was no actual proof, he too insisted my father had cancer. I know it seems absurd that all of these "experts" continued to believe Dad had a disease that science couldn't prove, but that's what happened. It seems they were using *cancer* as a blanket diagnosis because they could give no other reasonable explanation.

My frustration was mounting because I was unable to get some straight answers. I needed to get away for a few days, so Dena and I went to Hawaii to chill out. We partied hard, drinking Patrón, smoking Maui's best, and popping pills from the moment we arrived. I was in such deep denial about my father's illness that staying numb helped me cope.

I absolutely loved smoking weed. I never wanted to give it up. I always made sure I had enough to go around. I usually bought a quarter pound of smoke for friends and a quarter pound of kush, the good stuff, for my own use. The combination of popping pills, drinking without boundaries, and smoking was killing me, and the signs were there.

Things had gotten so bad that I could no longer even control my bodily functions. I was drinking around the clock, seven days a week—mostly beer but now I had started turning to hard alcohol to get even more buzzed. I drank so much that I began wetting my shorts several times a day. I looked down and realized, "This sucks." It was so uncool. I was too young to be peeing my pants.

I was always so wasted that I didn't even know how bad I really felt.

My hangovers gave me the shakes every morning. After we were back from Hawaii, I took Ativan and Xanax to level out so I could visit Dad without looking like death warmed over.

As a spiritual man, Dad refused to believe that God would have stricken him with such a horrible disease. His faith was unshakable. I kept questioning the medication they had him on, but no one gave any credibility to what I was saying.

As Dad got worse, it was obvious something was killing him, but still no one could really confirm the cancer diagnosis. Ultimately his body turned on itself. He no longer had the resistance to fight whatever was eating away at him. The doctors wanted to start Dad on chemotherapy, and reluctantly he agreed. I told him I thought it would be worth going through with the chemo if it would get him better. After his first treatment, he took a turn for the worse and was placed in the Intensive Care Unit. Even after that, I wouldn't give any weight to the idea that he could die. I hired the top doctors I could find. I just believed they would fix Dad.

Toward the end, Dad got really bad. He had gnarly bedsores and was in absolute agony. I asked the doctor to please give him something to ease his discomfort. They would only give him Ativan, which I was well aware was enough to relax him but not enough to kill the pain. He needed something stronger but never got it.

I spent a total of forty days and nights watching my father slowly, painfully slip away. I was at his bedside when he took his last breath. It was a single gasp for air.

I helplessly watched as nurses attached tubes and wires to his chest and body trying to revive him. They shocked his chest with paddles to get his heart started again. It was a frightening and chaotic scene, something I'd only seen on television. I was mesmerized—frozen from shock.

The doctors and nurses scurried around trying to bring my father back to life. All I could hear was the loud monotone beep coming from one of the monitors behind him. He had flatlined.

I couldn't take it.

I hovered over the sink in his room as I began to dry heave and cry as hard as I ever have in my life. I couldn't believe what was happening.

I walked out of the room just as my father's wife, Mindi, was approaching. She didn't know what had happened, and I didn't want to be the one to tell her, but I had to.

"He's dead." I could barely utter those two words.

My father was married to Mindi for eighteen years. They worked together running a mini storage business. In their spare time, they'd often visit jails to play music for the inmates to help uplift their spirits. They were the type of couple that was never apart. I never knew any other couple in my life that could spend as much time together as they did and still be happy. It was never Dad alone. It was always Reggie and Mindi. They were truly two souls that had become like one.

Mindi was there every day, by my father's side. Dad died in the few minutes she had left to get something to eat. She began

Dad and my stepmom, Mindi.

to cry, asking why she wasn't there. Why, on this day, was she not with Dad? I couldn't answer her. Maybe he wanted to spare her the pain of watching him slip away. I guess we'll never really know.

Through her tears, Mindi turned to me and said, "There's one thing your dad wanted more than anything else in this world, Reggie. And that was for you to accept Jesus Christ into your heart."

I was listening to her every word, though I have to admit I wasn't ready to hear what she was saying. I didn't even know what her words meant. I didn't know anything about spirituality or religion. Up until that moment, my world had only been about me.

"Pray with me, Reggie." She was adamant. I didn't know

what to say or do. I couldn't say no. We bowed our heads as Mindi began to pray.

"Father, I come to you in the name of your son, Jesus. I am a sinner. Please forgive me for all of my sins. Please come into my heart and be my Lord and my savior. Please fill me with your precious spirit and begin to set me free. Thank you for saving me. In the name of Jesus Christ, I pray, Amen."

I said that prayer completely unaware of how those words would touch my heart—and change my life in ways I was unable to imagine.

After Dad died, Jon came by to see me and pay his respects. It was the first chance he and I had to talk since losing Dad. I told him that I was sorry for not understanding what he went through when he lost his grandfather four years before. At the time, I didn't understand the pain of that type of loss so I didn't know to reach out and be there for my good friend. I had never experienced death when Jon lost his grandfather so I had no clue of the pain he must have been feeling to make the decision to get clean and sober. But now that I had lost my dad, I completely understood what he went through. I wanted to let Jon know that even though I wasn't there for him then, I wanted to be there for him now. We gave each other a long hug. I thanked him for coming over. It was strange to bond over something like death. I hadn't felt that close to Jon for years. I was grateful for his love and support and will never forget his compassion.

I thought about that visit for days. I realized I had done the same thing to Munky when his mom died. I didn't reach out like I should have, so I called him up to let him know that I was sorry I wasn't there for him. I tried to explain that I wasn't in a place in my own life at the time when she died to understand that he needed his friends around him. I didn't get it then, but I did now. I think he appreciated my sincerity. It definitely came from my heart.

A week went by between Dad's passing and his funeral, which was held in Bakersfield. Everything seemed so weird to me. I was having an especially hard time processing my own emotions on losing Dad. I had become very good at masking my pain, hiding my emotions, and running from myself. I spent most of that week partying until I was numb. I didn't want to feel a thing.

Me and Jon.

On the day of the funeral, I was amazed at the number of people who came to pay their last respects. The pastor was a friend of Dad's whom I had never met. He was a black dude who was dressed sort of hip-hop style, wearing a white hat low over his head and was dressed kind of pimped out. I wondered what he was all about. He looked a little ghetto, but really cool. He was so alive and funny—I almost couldn't believe what I was seeing. His presence stood in stark contrast to the sadness that filled the church.

Much to my surprise, Head also came to the funeral. It almost seemed like there was a glow all around him. Everything else was like tunnel vision around him as he slowly approached me that day. Head was crying as he spoke.

He said, "You know there's one thing your dad really wanted for you. He wished you could accept and have Jesus in your heart."

I stared back at Head as he spoke. For some reason, I was really pissed off by what he was saying.

"How do you know I don't have Jesus in my heart?" I shot back. I didn't want to hear Head preach to me. Not that day. Not at my dad's funeral. I turned and walked away.

I still had to give the eulogy and didn't want to be angry when I spoke. I've always hated speaking in front of a crowd. It's funny that playing music to large groups never bothered me, but public speaking always made me nervous. Even so, I found the courage to stand in front of the crowd that had gathered to remember Dad and celebrate his life. When I got up to read a letter I had written, I may have appeared focused and thoughtful, but I was a complete mess. I was still out of my mind in the craziest, darkest place I'd ever been. I probably wouldn't have written the same letter today, but in 2005, this is where my heart was at.

"My dad was one of the coolest dudes I've ever met, besides myself." I paused, waiting for the crowd to laugh. "He truly walked the walk."

Dad would tell me, "Son, I'm the same guy. I just took all of the sin out of my life." At the time, I had no idea what that meant. I knew Dad was a good Christian man who never judged me for anything I did that was against the way he lived his life.

I continued, and said, "I asked Dad why people had to act so stupid when they get saved. He told me when people are born again, they're like babies. The people I have seen get saved acted like fools for years, and then became really cool. There's no way I was going to act like a fool. If you truly walk the walk, your family and friends will follow. Once you have the respect from the people you want it from, you can try and save the world, but it's not going to happen overnight. Just because you're saved doesn't mean you're better than everyone. You still have to be a part of this world and live in it." I read what I wrote without hearing the words I spoke.

I stood silent for another moment before I looked up from the crinkled notebook paper I had written these words on. "If Dad had one favor left, I'm sure he would have said to drop all of the family fights and personal fights and love one another for the individuals that we are."

As nervous as I was, I somehow managed to pull the speech off like I was Mr. Confidence. Whatever Dad had had, now more than ever, it was painfully clear I wasn't spiritually where I needed to be. I wanted what Dad had possessed—his inner peace. The dude was always happy. Dad had been able to put himself in any situation, and thrive. I wanted that. My life had come to a point where I was continually deteriorating, downward spiraling and out of control. I couldn't stay straight long enough to see how messed up things had become.

Dad knew that I drank, smoked weed, and popped pills. For years, he saw that I was a mess, but he never once damned me to hell for my actions. He just continued to show me unconditional love. I knew he didn't like the way I was living my life, but he never judged me or made me feel like a loser for my decisions.

There was one time, a few years back when Dad tried to broach the subject, but it ended up pushing me away. He told me he realized that tact wouldn't work with me so he just loved me for who I was and where I was at in my life. He said, "Son, there's only one gift in this world that never fails . . . and that's love." I have never forgotten those words. He was right, and in his death, he gave me the most amazing gift a father could leave to his son. He opened my eyes.

After the wake and funeral, Dena and I made the two-and-a-half-hour drive from Bakersfield back to Laguna. We pulled over at a rest stop to smoke a joint as the sun was setting. We were both quiet. It had been a long day. I had just buried my father. There really wasn't a lot to say. I was truly heartbroken about losing my dad. I lost my best friend when he died.

Fifteen of us went back to my house after the funeral. At the time, I kept beer stocked in every possible corner of my house. I had refrigerators in my kitchen, pantry, backyard, garage, and studio that were all stocked with beer. When we came home, everyone headed straight to the refrigerators to grab a drink for themselves. One by one, I heard the cracking sound as each can was opened. I remember thinking, *Can everyone not drink today . . . out of respect for my dad?* I'm not sure if I ever voiced that aloud, but I'll never forget feeling that way.

There was such darkness over my home that night. I didn't really want to make an issue out of everyone's drinking, but I couldn't be around it, either. I went upstairs to my room to be alone. I felt a presence watching over me that night. In the depths of my grief, I was comforted by that presence. I wasn't sure what it was, but I was grateful for its existence.

Later that night Dena; her sister Kristy; my stepmother, Mindi; and I all found ourselves in the guestroom where Mindi was staying. I had asked her to come home with us because I didn't want her to be alone. We talked for a while. Everyone seemed calm and at peace. Once again, Mindi asked if we'd like to pray with her. We got into a circle and prayed together. Mindi said the same prayer as she did in the hospital. She prayed—I listened. This time, it was different. I felt cold and got the chills. It was overwhelming. We all felt the same thing. When we were done praying, Mindi was inexplicably excited. It was weird and a lot for me to take in. I thought she was some kind of nut. I couldn't understand what she was so excited about. I didn't dwell on it. I just said good night and went to bed. I thought about Dad all night. I did what I thought he'd do. I prayed to Jesus for help to stop partying.

The next morning, I pulled out my bong, like I did every morning for as long as I could remember, and took a big long rip. Wake and bake. That's all I knew. I looked in the mirror, watching myself get high. Something told me I was going to die of cancer from smoking weed if I didn't stop. I wasn't ready to give up weed. I loved getting high—but I wasn't ready to die, either. I didn't want to be the cliché rock star found dead from an accidental overdose.

Later that day, I went to my safe where I kept my stash and

started pulling it all out. There was probably a good pound of five or six different types of pot in there. I walked over to the toilet and dumped it all. There was so much weed in the bowl that I wasn't even sure the toilet would flush. I stared at the green muck for a moment and without hesitation pushed the lever down, watching the swirl of pot slowly disappear. That was it. I was done.

Shortly after that, Dena called me to dinner. She had my usual Corona set up at the table. She made Mexican that night. I could never resist a cold beer with Mexican food, but for some reason, I wasn't interested in drinking. Not then, not ever again. And that was the end of my drinking.

I went to bed that night well aware that I needed to change all of my bad habits. Something kept telling me that I needed to turn to someone greater than me. Fieldy's Rules no longer worked. I spent most of the night lying in bed thinking about God and Jesus. I prayed with all of my heart.

"Am I really done? Help me God, because if I am really done, I'm going to need your help." I knew I didn't have the strength to get through this all alone. It would definitely take the intervention of a higher power to help me maintain my sobriety. I don't know how or why I figured that out. Looking back, it had to be the help of the Lord.

The next day, I woke up, same as I always did. But this time, I had no craving for alcohol or drugs. My mind-set had been changed. It was like ending a relationship that you knew was already done. It was easy to walk away from drugs and alcohol because I could see it was killing me. Miraculously, I had no withdrawals, no shakes, nothing.

I had spent twenty years, seven days a week, filling my mind and body with toxins. Suddenly, my desire to feel that way was gone. I continued to take Xanax for a few weeks, but that felt wrong, too, so I stopped cold turkey. I kept praying for the Lord to help me so I wouldn't be tempted to go back to my old ways. *Ask, and ye shall receive.*

Everyone around me doubted my intentions, thinking my newfound sobriety was a passing phase I was going through. So many people. But I was committed to staying clean. I didn't let what other people thought or believed sway me from my path. If I weren't so strong in my mind and conviction, it might have been more of a struggle to face down those demons and doubters. There was nothing anyone could say, though, that would change my mind or my destiny.

I had been set free from the bondages I was in—sort of. There was still my guilt to deal with.

After I got sober, I spent a solid year apologizing for all the bad things I did. I prayed every night that the Lord would forgive me for being so mean and cruel over the years. I pleaded, saying I didn't know any better. My intentions were never bad, but after a twelve-pack and some weed, I'd inevitably rip you apart. Three beers in, my mouth turned into some kind of weapon, filled with cuss words and anger. And you'd better hope your wife was nowhere in sight because I would have gone for her if I was messed up. And how many times on the road did I find some random girl, take her to the back of the tour bus, have sex with her, and make one of my security guys throw her out after I was done? Just like that. It was so cold. It was no way to live. My consequences were pure hell. I never had peace in my life. Never. That sucked. I never felt comfortable, safe, or loved. If getting stoned were better, I'd still be doing it.

As I prayed for forgiveness, I promised the Lord that I would never go back to being that guy. Coming clean was hard. I knew there were plenty of people I had to apologize to, but I had no idea there were so many people out there I barely knew, hating me for being a drunken fool—but there were.

Korn was invited to play the KROQ Acoustic Christmas show a few years back. Someone came up to me and said that this guy, Steve O from *Jackass,* hated me. This dude was telling people he wanted to fight me because I wouldn't shake his hand at a party a few years back. I couldn't remember ever meeting him, let alone dissing him like that. I thanked the guy for telling me and tried to apologize by explaining those types of situations are part of the reason I don't drink anymore. What a waste of energy, man. I would never disrespect someone like that sober. That was my usual explanation, and for the most part, people were being pretty cool in accepting.

There's a quote from Proverbs in the Bible that says, "An offended friend is harder to win back than a fortified city. Arguments separate friends like a gate locked with bars." Man, did I discover how true that is. Some people accepted my apology like it was no big deal. Others heard me out, but refused to believe I had really changed. In their eyes, I was branded a jerk for life. There wasn't a lot I could do to change their mind except stay steady on my newfound path and walk my talk.

I wrote the following letters to my bandmates while writing this book. They have not seen or read them prior to the book going to print. I tried to talk to each of them after getting sober, to somehow let them know I was truly sorry for the mistakes I had made over the years. I'm not sure I ever really conveyed how much regret I had, or how important each of those guys really is to me. The letters took me several months to draft, but each came pouring out of me once I found the right words and the sentiment I wanted to share.

Dear Brian (Head)—

I'm writing your letter first because I've known you the longest. First thing I would like to say is, I read your book and I think you did a good job and I'm proud of you. But reading your book brought back some memories of some of the things I did to you. Looking back, I wish things would have been a lot different. I especially wish I hadn't said so many things to hurt you.

I know now that a physical beating would have healed better than the things I said to you. Please forgive me for all the hurtful hell I put you through. I didn't know any better. I was just living my life with free will. The only time I would listen to you was through your fingers when they would talk on your guitar. And when your fingers were talking, I liked everything you had to say. I still think you're one of the best musicians in the world.

I know you turned your life around and I want you to know that I have turned mine around, too. If we ever hang out in our new lives, we will both have gray hair faster than Just for Men could cover it. I know we would hold each other accountable and make some amazing changes in the world.

Today, you don't know me, but I'll tell you what: I would be the best friend you've ever had. I hope we can find a way to make that happen.

Love, your friend,
Fieldy

Dear Jon—

You are such a cool rock star. When you take the stage, I feel your energy. The uniqueness of your voice makes it one of my favorites and what blows me away is that on stage you are a madman with this powerful voice. I also feel like a proud dad watching you grow lyrically.

Most singers I've known or heard about are egomaniacs. Not you. Offstage, you are this humble dude that likes to help people with their bags, even help push equipment. Because you are such a passive guy, I would lash out at you, but you would never react. So I gave up on you and lashed out on everyone you cared about and loved. I had no idea I was hurting you. I was just drunk and on pills.

I was an out-of-control punk that thought, "This is how a rock star is supposed to live." I've made a big change in my life and want you to know that I am no longer here to tear people down. It feels so good to build people up. You are amazing to me and I love to learn from your good qualities.

I'm now capable of being a better friend. We've got to tear down the walls and use the bricks to build bridges. It takes years to build a bridge. I love the work and got nothing but time. I'm thankful and excited to keep growing together.

Love,
Billy*

*For whatever reason, Jon has called me Billy for as long as I can remember. Sometimes when I introduce myself to other people they think I tell them my name is Billy, so it has stuck with me.

Dear David—

Where did it all go wrong? I don't know if this
is where it started. But this is as far back as I can
remember. L.A.P.D. was trying to put together some
songs at our jam spot, but really never got anything
done, because we were all getting drunk and jamming
and singing five or six songs to the ten or fifteen
people that we invited down every night.

One night, I said something to piss you off. And you
said something to piss me off. The sad thing is, I don't
remember what was said. We blew it off and started
the song. During this three-minute song, I drank a
whole 40-ouncer of St. Ides malt liquor. And I was
seeing red. I made my mind up that at the end of this
song, we were going to fight. So, the song ended and
I threw my bass down and stepped off the stage and
called you out. I had my fists in the air.

And you looked like you were going to kill me. A lot
of screaming went down but no fight, thank God. I was
so drunk that I'm not sure of all the things I said, but
I'm sure it was hurtful because things haven't been
the same since. We would see each other for the next
twenty years and I would say, "Hey, what's up?" And
you would say, "Hey, what's up?" and that'd be it.

Looking back, I believe my actions bothered you
over the years. I was a pig. I would walk into the
dressing room and slam down half my beer and burp
as loud as possible on purpose and then leave the
beer half full so I could throw it against the wall and
watch it splatter everywhere. And then I'd spit, walk
over, take a bite of pizza, and throw that against the

other wall. Finally, I walked over and farted on our tour manager. Meanwhile, nobody could stop me or my mouth. I had nothing in common with you.

Fast-forward —several years later, I'm on my way to the nicest restaurant in town with my best outfit on, showered up and smelling good. And who do I see? You. I really enjoy nice restaurants. So, I start going out to eat every night on tour. And who do I see? You. I found that I really enjoy working out. So, I start going to the gym in the hotel or around town. And who do I see? You.

I could go on and on about how much we have in common. It's too bad things ended up the way they did—because we would've been—we could have been good friends today.

Love,
Fieldy

Dear James (Munky)—

I remember being in the airport several years ago getting ready to check in our bags. We were both still drunk from the night before. We exchanged some words that were what we always called "drunk talk."

I don't know what you said, but I was pissed. I pushed you as hard as I could. My Presidential Rolex snapped loose, so I slipped it off my wrist and handed it to Loc. Then I took off my huge, heavy gold chain around my neck, and punched you in the chest.

It was about to go down when Loc jumped between us, ending what could have been a very bad fight. In the Bible, Proverbs 20:1 says "Wine produces mockers; alcohol leads to brawls. Those led astray by drink cannot be wise." It was a stupid thing to do.

I think you've done a great job stepping up on the guitar. When Head left the band, for whatever reason, it brought out the best in you. I love to listen to your guitar work and I think you are one of the best showmen in the world. Thank you for taking the extra time in the studio to show me the new songs we create. You really go out of your way for me. You have made me such a better bass player these past few years.

I have three sisters and no brothers so you are like the brother I've never had. I've done more with you than any other member of Korn. When I look back, I choose to remember all the good times and block out the bad. Sorry for all the hell I've put you through. But man, I remember some fun times. From sharing an apartment in Long Beach, where I slept in a walk-in closet with a lamp and a single-sized mattress to making L.A.P.D. fliers and going down to the Sunset Strip to pass them out. And finally, waking up early in the morning to work down at the Glen Ivy, where we got people to sign up for a free trip to Hawaii when it was a scam to send people to a ninety-minute time-share seminar.

I could write a whole book on the lives of just Munky and Fieldy. We've had a lot of history together.

You have recently told me that I have put you through hell in the past. With all the pills and drinking I did, I don't remember much except a few fights. I know I once called you a "kiss ass" but today I can see that you are an understanding guy. I know that there are probably hundreds of situations that I was a jerk, but I can only recall the airport fight and calling you a kiss ass. And for all of that, I am sorry. If there are any other hurtful things I have done to you, please tell me about them if they are bothering you because I just can't remember.

I want you to know that I would never treat you the way that I used to in the past. Thank you for all of the good memories. I am your friend for the rest of our days. I love you James "Munky" Shaffer.

Reggie "Fieldy" Arvizu

Apologizing to peripheral people was a lot easier than confessing my guilt to those whom I truly loved. I saved those apologies for the bitter end, including the preceding letters. When I first got sober, I made it a point to reach out to my friend Loc to tell him I was sorry about what happened in Arizona. I apologized to all of my friends who might have been (and probably were) on the receiving end of one of my infamous "Fieldy's wraths" over the years—sometimes more than once. And finally, I had to apologize to Dena, the hardest confession of them all.

I had put it off as long as I possibly could, but my conscience was getting to me. I had to come clean and tell her the awful truth. It was the only way I could finally be at peace in my own life. I knew I could lose her with what I had to say, but my heart told me to tell her, anyway. I had always heard that the truth shall set you free—what they forget to tell you is that it will first make you miserable.

I finally worked up the courage to tell her everything as we lay in bed one night.

"There's something I've got to tell you . . ." Those words are never precursors to anything good.

"I have to do this, Dena, even though it's going to suck." She didn't say a word. I was doing all of the talking.

"You know I'm on the road a lot. When I'm on tour, I've been cheating on you." I could see her face drop in the darkness. She asked for details, which I didn't want to give.

"It's as bad as it gets, Dena. I was a pig and that's all you need to know." But that wasn't enough to satisfy her curiosity. I don't know why women need to know all of the intimate information, but I was in no position to negotiate so I told her everything. I told her about the nightly parties, the Chickenhead Room, and the escapades on my bus. I made it sound as out of control as it was because I didn't want her to think I was holding anything back. I loved Dena—but I still wasn't mature enough to understand that true love was anything different from what I was describing. That's how I always loved. I always cheated. It hadn't been a real problem in the past because I never had a woman I cared enough about to make it matter. Dena was different. There was something about her that made me want to stop cheating and dedicate my whole self to loving only her.

Dena didn't take the news very well. She turned into Linda Blair from *The Exorcist*. She started screaming and talking all crazy. Her voice became almost unrecognizable. I remember thinking she must have been possessed by demons because she was not herself—I had seen Dena go off plenty of times in the past, but the girl standing in front of me in this moment wasn't anyone I knew—or wanted to know. She grabbed things off the nightstand and threw them at me. She was absolutely losing her mind. I didn't know what to say or how to calm her down. I kept apologizing over and over hoping she would hear the sincerity in my words. There was nothing I could do except give her the time and space she would need to process and hopefully get over my revelation.

I had been prepared to go all the way that night with one other important confession that needed to take place before I could be completely free and clear in my heart and soul. However, given her reaction to the cheating, I wasn't ready to drop the final bomb on her just yet. I was getting ready to go on tour in a couple of weeks. I decided to write her a letter that contained my final admission. I hid the letter in between some T-shirts in my closet so she wouldn't accidentally find it before I was ready to confess.

A little while into the tour, I decided the time had come to finally come completely clean with Dena. I loved her so much, I owed her the truth. I called her from the road and told her there was something else she needed to know. I explained to her that I wanted to tell her in person but was afraid to. The truth is, I didn't want to tell her at all, but I had to because every night I laid my head down it was the only thing left in my conscience holding me back from being completely free. I wanted peace in my life. We spoke for a few minutes before I guided her on where to find the letter and hung up.

Dear Dena—

I'm writing you this letter to tell you that I love you with all my heart and I want to spend the rest of my life with you. I think about you so much. You are the one for me and the one who makes me feel every emotion. Without you, my life would be dull. I need to feel more than just happy.

Thanks for making me feel pissed off, sad, lonely, frustrated, motivated, lovable, and happy.

Now it is time for your heart to drop into your stomach. There is something I have wanted to tell you but it hasn't been the right time. After I tell you this I will be completely set free and my record will be clean with you and God. I hope that you can laugh at that or understand I was messed up.

One night I was really messed up and I was on pills, weed, and a lot of alcohol. I felt like the devil— for real. I walked into your sister's room—it was when her room was in Sarina and Olivia's room. (I want you to know that I am not leaving out any of the details.) She was in bed and I pulled the covers back and said, "Let me see your butt." I pulled down her pants or lifted up her skirt (I don't remember) and said, "Your butt is tan." She said, "You're wasted. Get out." Then I think I said, "Let me see if your tits are tan." I was being aggressive. I felt like Satan. She kept telling me to get out, so I did. That is every detail of that night.

But the next day or a few days later (I don't remember), she was laying out. I went over to her and told her that one day she would be able to tell you what happened. Again, I was high, so I said, "One day you will be able to tell your sister what happened. I wish you had more of a story to tell her than I just looked at your butt! I wish something more happened, but if you tell Dena, I will just deny it and kick you out."

But out of all that, I did tell her I was sorry. And I want you to know I don't find your sister attractive at all. I was just upset, wasted, and without God in my life. I'm sorry for everything I've done to you but it wasn't personal. But if you want a man that you can trust and that will never cheat on you or even flirt and that's trying to live the right life with you and God, then I'm the right guy. I think about you and only you. I just want to have a family with you and grow old together and die together. But, for the rest of our time together, I want you to know I stand for the truth. I love you, Dena. You have nothing to worry about ever again.

> Love,
> Fieldy

Dena read the letter and called me back. She was screaming and crying. This time I was totally flipping out because I knew how much my words must have hurt. She said she always suspected something between her sister and me but had purposely kept herself in denial. I didn't want to hurt Dena. I told her how sorry I was—over and over again. I kept saying that this was the reason I could no longer drink or take drugs. I would never have done anything like that sober. It took some time for Dena to realize that I had really changed and that none of the things I apologized for would ever happen again.

It took a lot of repairing, but we eventually got through it. I had to change every facet of myself to become a better man. Dena hasn't seen the pig I was in years. I changed everything about my actions—what I said, where I looked, and who I talked to. I won't even cuss anymore because it's a negative way of communicating.

It sounds simple, but reprogramming who I am was one of the hardest things I have ever done. I now wake up every day thinking of ways to have fun, laugh, and be positive. I just want to have a good time in life like I always did, except this time around, I want to do it sober.

Once Dena realized my changes were real and that I am truly a changed man, she knew I'd never intentionally hurt her again. Even so, building back trust in our relationship took time. The first time I went back on tour after confessing all of this was really hard for her. She didn't trust me at all. I totally understood, but I had to constantly remind her that I didn't change for her. I changed because of my fear of the Lord. I knew He was watching every little move I made so I had to act right or I'd have a higher power than my girlfriend to answer to.

When I prayed and asked the Lord for help, I didn't know I had opened that door all the way. At first I thought the Lord would just help me find the strength to quit drinking. Then I thought it was just to help me stay loyal to my girl. I didn't know He's an all-or-nothing proposition.

So I didn't fear Dena. I feared the Lord. If I only feared her, I'd probably be doing the same old thing, cheating and sneaking around on tour. But things were different. Now I had someone else looking over my shoulder 24/7. The Holy Spirit came into my life like some imaginary friend who follows you around wherever you go, watching everything you do. If I did something wrong, He'd be right there shaking his head letting me know He didn't approve. We all have an inner spirit. God placed it in each of us. It's that little voice that says, "This is wrong." Some of us pay attention to it while others don't.

Along with this inner spirit, God gave each of us free will, which is the power to choose to override the spirit. I spent years overriding my inner voice. Thankfully, I no longer fight the angel and the devil on my shoulders. It's really the same idea as feeding the good or bad dog. Call it intuition, conscience, God, or spirit— it's a gift that God gave each of us to help guide us through the right and wrong in life.

Do I sometimes fall short? Every single day, but I try my best to slow down and pay attention to it so I can better my life.

I think I'm a work in progress, and I'm doing the best I know how to right now. I know I will still hurt people, even let them down from time to time, because I am only human. No matter how wrong I am, I will always apologize with all my heart. And, if someone wrongs me, I will forgive them with all of my heart.

When Head wrote his book a few years back, the idea of it shook the rest of us guys in the band. I remember standing backstage one night when Jonathan said he wanted to knock Head out because he had heard he was writing a tell-all book about Korn. Jon called it a "snitch" book.

One of the other guys blurted out, "That's not very Christian of Head! I thought Christians are supposed to love everybody."

Jon is a really sweet guy. I knew he didn't mean what he was saying because he'd probably end up hugging it out with Head instead of punching him out. At the end of the day we all loved one another—whether he was still in the band or not. I knew Head's book may not have been what we wanted, and it might not have been right to do. But if Head believed it was right in his heart, then it made it right. After all, if it was intentionally hurtful and malicious, then I knew Head would have to answer the consequences down the road. I didn't want the book to hurt us, but I knew I could forgive Head if it did.

In the end, his book wasn't anything to be upset about. The man shared his personal journey and I think he did a good job. There wasn't any negative fallout for anyone.

There hasn't been a moment since I got sober where I haven't thought about why Head left the band or his words to me that day at my dad's funeral. I wish he was back with Korn because I never got to hang out with him sober. Now that we are both sober we could make some unbelievable music together. We could also hang out with each other on a different level than we ever have, and develop a new sense of friendship. I hope we get that chance someday.

GOT THE LIFE

After Dad died, I found myself frequently thinking back to something he said to me many times over the years: "The one gift that never fails is love." For the first time in my life, I finally understood what that truly meant. I had completely come clean with Dena about all of my infidelities and was able to clear my conscience so I could enter into the holy sanctity of marriage free of any guilt from my past. I spent two weeks answering every question she had about the who, what, where, and when of my indiscretions. My candid truth and brutal honesty was more than she (or anyone) could be expected to handle. The relationship was definitely in jeopardy, and this time, it looked like it would be for good.

Looking back, why would anyone want to stay with a guy who had a history of being so disrespectful of his relationships? I couldn't blame her for wanting to leave. If she had been a tiny bit as indiscreet as I had been, I would

The two become one—Dena and me on our wedding day.

have told her to hit the road. I was heartbroken from losing my dad and now I faced losing the only woman I have ever really truly loved.

Despite my every effort to put the pieces of our relationship back together, Dena made up her mind. It was over. I help-lessly watched as she packed up her things. The entire pro-cess was overwhelming for both of us. In a last-ditch effort to salvage things, I suggested taking a vacation—nothing fancy, just a road trip to Bakersfield to see my mom. Okay, I'll admit, it wasn't the most romantic gesture. I probably should have said, "Let's go to Hawaii or Tahiti." Any remote place where we could iron things out would have been better than Bakers-field. But I wanted to go home to see Mom and tell her what was happening. The little boy in me needed that nurturing that only my mother could provide. I genuinely thought some time away would be good for the relationship and that maybe I could convince Dena to give me another chance. Much to my surprise, she agreed to take the ride north with me.

She was having a rough time with the reality of my confes-sions the entire trip. She cried nonstop. In an effort to bring some levity to the situation, I took her to Dave's Tacos, my fa-vorite Mexican joint in Bakersfield for carryout. We took our meal home and sat in my mother's backyard in the rain eating tacos, trying to be normal. Earlier that day, I told my mother I had confessed everything to Dena. It felt really good to let her know that I was trying to clean up the trail of destruction I'd spent twenty or more years creating. I told Mom how bad I felt about the way I treated Dena. I found myself going on and on about what a good person she is and how I didn't want to lose her. The more I spoke, the louder that little voice inside my head got, saying, "Don't let her go."

Dena had stood by me through the worst of times. Now

that the tide was turning, I wanted her to share my new life and faith because I knew the best was yet to come. I decided that I had to ask her to marry me. I wasn't feeling pressured like I had in my past relationships. My heart was certain this was what I had to do even though I didn't have a ring or a plan about what to say. Even so, I wasn't absolutely sure I would go through with it until I spontaneously got down on one knee.

I was well aware that Dena knew all about my past failures and general ambivalence toward marriage. I was pretty clear throughout our relationship that marriage wasn't an option. It never seemed to bother her that I felt that way because she was so young and overall we had a pretty good thing going. But now, I had come to a place in my life where I had no choice but to follow my heart. It was a risk, but one worth taking.

As I knelt down, I could see Dena had no idea what was going on. And then, I heard Mom gasp and say, "I know what he's about to do!" That's when it must have clicked in with Dena, too.

It all happened so fast. I said something like "You're the only woman I want to be with. I love you so much. I am really sorry about everything I've done and all that I've put you through. Will you marry me?"

She didn't answer at first. She just stared at me in what I can only describe as total disbelief. My heart pounded in anticipation of her response. And then she said, "For real?"

I nodded yes.

But still, she didn't give me an answer. I began to sweat as I watched her thinking it through. She was obviously still mad at me. I was hoping she would see that getting over her hurt feelings would be better than losing what we had. I was making irreversible changes and wanted Dena by my side for the rest of my life. Seconds ticked by, but it felt like hours. Finally, she said . . . "Yes."

On May 11, 2005, Dena made me the happiest man in the world when she agreed to marry me. She ribbed me a little for not having a ring when I proposed, but I thought she'd like a say in the ring she'd wear as my wife. It took us nine months to find the perfect ring, but when we did, I knew she'd wear it forever.

I was on a new path in life, one that made lots of people very happy and many people extremely uncomfortable. Everything around me was changing and it was becoming rather obvious to my closest friends and family that I was becoming a very different guy.

I was in a desperate search for answers. I knew that getting sober wasn't my end game; I needed to change my entire life. I thought back to my childhood when my parents tried to guide me along the way. Like most rebellious teenagers, I didn't trust them. I couldn't understand why Mom and Dad thought they could tell me how to act—that their way was the right way to do things. There were many times I can think back on when Dena tried to tell me that I needed Jesus in my life. Usually the subject came up after a long night of partying, while we were both wasted. I would cuss at her and freak out at the mere mention of His name. I had no idea why I got so angry. How can you be mad at something you don't understand? But I was—often.

I spent most of my adult life insisting there be no sign of religious affiliation around me. I didn't know anything about God, Jesus, or the Bible, so I feared all of it. There were never crosses in my homes or around my neck. I even told Dena she wasn't allowed to wear one in my presence. If she was wearing a cross around her neck, I always made her take it off. My father once gave me a set of gold praying hands bookends. I didn't say anything when he gave them to me. Instead, I just stashed them in my garage for a week or two before throwing them out. Man, looking back on that makes me so sad today because those were a gift from my father, something that can never be replaced now that he's gone.

Shortly after Dad died, Mindi gave me my first bible. I put it in my nightstand for a month or so. I thought about the peace Dad had later in his life. Seeing him so happy and content left an unforgettable impression on me. I knew he used the book for life guidance. If it worked for him, I thought it could work for me.

So one day I decided to do something I swore I'd never do. I pulled the Bible from the drawer and began reading it. I never had any specific religious background or affiliation with a church, so this was all new to me. The first words I read were "Man cannot live by bread alone but by every word that comes from the mouth of God." Suddenly, I understood what that meant. If you want to live a better life, you have to live by God's words. We're here for such a short amount of time. I wanted to make the most of the time I had left. I no longer had a desire to waste another moment.

I started reading God's word every day for the next year or so, until I read the entire book from beginning to end. Maybe it was Dad's legacy that inspired me to begin reading the Bible or perhaps it was the hand of God Himself directing me to follow His teachings. It didn't matter what brought me to this place. I was just so grateful to finally be there. My father never identified himself as a religious man and neither did I—ever. Dad's commitment to his faith was more about reading and living by God's words than it was practicing a specific religion. That made a lot of sense to me as I began my own journey to learning a better way.

The New Testament has become my guide to life. It brings me more wisdom, love, and understanding than anything else I have ever come across. I like reading books by guys like Joel Osteen that are inspirational messages rooted in my faith, but nothing is better than reading the Bible.

For some reason, the more I read, the clearer things became. Every word resonated as being the truth, the whole truth, and nothing but the truth. There was no doubt in my mind that what I was reading was the greatest handbook for life. The more I read, the better the stories got, too. There were stories on love, incest, killing, betrayal, and adultery. I was tripping out at how contemporary the themes were given the text was thousands of years old. The Bible was like reading a great suspense novel I couldn't put down. The stories from the Old Testament were fascinating and intense. I had heard of Moses and Noah, but I had never read about them. By the time I reached the New Testament, I was completely hooked.

By the time I finished the New Testament, everything became crystal clear. Life was no longer complicated. It was simple because every single answer to life's dilemmas was in those pages.

The Bible became my new addiction. I read it every day, slowly and methodically making my way through every story, trying hard to understand their messages and significance and how I could apply those lessons to my life. Like working out, reading the Bible daily took time and commitment. If I had approached it as a "task" or "chore," I would have never made it through the first few stories. I had to take my time so I could absorb every word. If I didn't understand something, I looked it up. There was no point to glazing over something, because every word was important.

One thing I learned in the process was that you will never

learn everything all at once. Each time I read the Bible, I picked up on something new. The words might have been the same but the significance or the message changed depending on what was happening in my life at the time. That is still true. The Bible isn't really about religion. It's about God's words, and His words are the absolute undeniable truth. You can't disagree with what you read because the buck stops there. That gave me lots to think about along the way.

Who was I to argue with God?

Once I figured out that His word was the final say, it was easy to give myself over to His teachings.

I'll admit that sin is fun. I loved to sin, but I realized there was no way I could handle the consequences I continually had to pay for my sin. It was obvious that I had to replace it with something better. I've said this before; if living a life of sin were better, I'd still be doing it. I no longer wanted to carry the weight of my guilt and shame on my shoulders. The Bible showed me there was a way out. I never felt like I was reading a religious book. It was more than that.

Whenever I was faced with a challenging situation during my recovery, I made it a habit to pause and ask God for help. I found myself praying to God every single day. I just wanted all of my unhealthy habits gone. As strange as it may seem, once I gave up alcohol and drugs, I never had a genuine urge or craving to go backward. I was done. I didn't go to any fancy rehab or use drugs to get me off booze and pills. I turned my need over to God and trusted that He would protect me from myself. If you really pray, and believe what you are saying without any doubt, it will be done for you.

I had blind faith from the moment I turned my life over to God. It was almost childlike in the way I trusted Him. I was at the end of my rope. I didn't want to keep living on the treadmill I had been on for all of those years. I felt half dead. I asked God to take my addiction away from me and never bring it back again. I was really specific when I prayed. Every word was intentional. Eventually, daily prayer became a daily part of my life, so much so that I don't think of it as any big deal anymore.

I haven't had a single drop of alcohol and have remained completely drug free since 2005. I could never have done it without God's help. I never related to AA or rehab. Although those types of programs might work for some people, my belief is that they would have been a setup for failure for a guy like me. I needed to find my path in my own time and on my own terms so I did whatever it took to stay focused and clean. I knew I couldn't do it alone. My friends who have been through rehab have tried to explain the process to me. In my mind, people who run those twelve-step programs are trying to play God—saying you *have* to get sober. Who are these people to be playing God? Ultimately, it is a losing proposition because there is really only one higher power. See how good your life works when you try being God.

I did it for years, playing only by Fieldy's Rules. I was living life on my terms without a care in the world for anyone else. It doesn't work. At least, it didn't for me until I surrendered myself and placed my life in the hands of the one and only God. Only then did miraculous changes begin to happen.

To me, coming to that realization was pretty simple. Every answer I had been seeking was contained within the pages of my Bible. It was as if someone had given me the recipe to make the perfect cake or a construction manual to build a better life. There was no way I could go wrong if I followed God's words. A lot of people think the Bible is all deep and crazy, but it's not. It's just a manual for life.

I know that if I ever lost my faith in God or stopped reading the Bible, I could easily fall away from the track I'm on. I don't go to church often, but when I do, it's usually to hear the good message at the end of the service. For whatever reason, I know God wants me to hear what the pastor has to say, so I always try to find the positive in the sermon.

I don't believe that God actually talks to people, but I do embrace His messages. He gave each of us a gift: His words in the form of the good book, the Bible. Now that I read His word every day, I never feel alone.

I've learned that I can't do anything completely on my own. And to be totally honest, I don't want to. I ask God for help with most everything. I used to believe I didn't need anyone for anything, but now I know, without a doubt, that is not true. The Bible says that you can accomplish anything with the faith of a mustard seed. I didn't know what that meant before I got sober. God is an almighty God. He created the universe and knows everything He placed in this world. Once I grasped that knowledge, I never wanted to let go.

There's a scripture that I have memorized because it is so meaningful to me. It comes from 1 Corinthians 10:13 and it says, "If you think you're standing strong, be careful not to fall. The temptations in your life are no different from what others experience. And God is faithful. He will not allow the temptation to be more than you can stand. When you are tempted, He will show you a way out so that you can endure."

I've always loved that because it makes it very clear that we all have the choice to get up and leave if we're uncomfortable. There's always a way out. It's what I refer to as before free will. It is up to you to realize you're in a bad situation and make the choice to leave, change, do whatever it takes to get out. I think that most people don't think through their choices all the way. They have to stop and ask themselves, "What is going to come from this?" Most people just think in terms of right now: "This is fun"; "I'll deal with the consequences tomorrow"; "No one will know."

You have to think every situation through because you are not promised a tomorrow. How many times did I wake up the morning after partying and regret my actions?

Too many to count.

When you do something that makes you feel bad afterward, it's time to stop doing that. When it comes to feeling bad, the consequences never justify the actions.

Coming off drugs and alcohol takes time and retraining to live in the world. When you're trying to get straight, it's a time of selfish reflection. Once I cleared my conscience from all of my misdeeds, I began to ask God for help in maintaining my new lifestyle. I became more aware of my faults and imperfections and worked hard to retrain my brain. It wasn't just about getting sober—I wanted to change everything about my life. For example, I stopped interrupting people when they spoke. I had to remind myself that sometimes people pause when they're talking and they're not quite finished. I realized I had a bad habit of cutting people off, which was constantly being misconstrued as being uninterested in what they were saying. That wasn't the case. I just jumped in to get my viewpoint across. I've since learned to listen and then speak. It has changed my entire perception of what people say because it forces me to absorb their every word.

Now that I'm a pretty good guy, people get a kick out of when I mess up. I can still hurt people with my words or tone of voice, but I am aware of it and keep trying to become a better communicator. That's a daily struggle for me, but one I am willing to face until it is no longer an issue.

I get the haters that gang up on me saying, "I thought you were Christian. You're a fake, a hypocrite." I've learned not to care about what other people think of me. God is my one and only judge. I'm confident that my commitment is strong, but I'm also human so it doesn't mean I won't mess up along the way.

People spend far too much time worrying about things that never come to pass. Someone once told me that 85 percent of the things we worry about never happen. What is the point in worrying about tomorrow or yesterday? We need to live in the moment. Today is all you need. There's not even a promise of tomorrow so what's the point in worrying about it?

When I look at other people around me who are struggling with addictions, I realize that most people see a backslide as failure, a letdown, and a major disappointment. If you're not strong in your conviction to being sober, you will use that momentary lapse as an excuse to go back to your old ways instead of seeing it as a mistake and getting right back on your righteous path. It's a struggle, but getting sober is worth the battle.

Being good doesn't come easy. You have to work at becoming good, which is a long and tedious process. It's no different from being bad—that takes work, too. You have to decide where you want to put your efforts. It's really as simple as that.

I know it can be challenging to shift the course when everyone else around you hasn't gotten onboard. Take it from me. Your real friends won't try to tempt you. For the most part, I still have a lot of the same friends I had before I got sober. Some have chosen to clean up their lives while others aren't quite there yet.

When I gave up alcohol and drugs, my friends were no-where near the end of their partying days. It didn't matter to me. They were free to do whatever they chose. That is why God gave each of us free will. If someone told me to get sober, there would have been no way I would have listened. You have to make that choice for yourself. No one else can make it for you and you can't make someone else choose for themselves if they aren't truly ready for the change. It is a setup for failure.

I have found that when I tell my friends no, they shrug their shoulders and move on. And you know what? They're still my friends. Anytime someone tries to convince me that one beer or one toke is no big deal, I use that opportunity to tell them how happy I am without drugs and alcohol. I have been looking for that joy my entire life. I don't preach or pontificate about my reasons. I simply state where I'm at. I never tell someone not to drink or cuss around me, but my actions make them think I do.

It's true when they say that actions really do speak louder than words.

Since I've learned to live strong, my actions are louder than any words. Life has become such an adventure filled with so much pleasure that people can feel it emanating from me. They don't know how to describe it other than to say there is a peace that now surrounds me. That elusive peace I have always been seeking is now a part of me. I don't tell people how to live—I just let them watch how I live and think, "I want what that dude has." It's so much better to go against the flow and blaze your own trail than it is to be in a pack of sheep following the leader. No one knows what is right for you except you.

Timing is everything.

People make the choice to get sober for all sorts of reasons. The motivation isn't as important as the outcome. But it sure seems like something dramatic always happens to finally push you over. For me, it took losing my dad to see I needed to change or I would probably die, too. I've had friends who got sober because they didn't want to end up like other dudes they saw who messed up their lives. I was never that type of conformist. I always needed to see proof of things for myself.

It took me years to place my trust in something that is actually worthy—something that has stood the test of time. I no longer lean on my own understanding of things. I don't have to. I trust in the Lord's guidance. I guess you could say I found blind faith, the ability to believe in what I can't actually see. I don't have the same strong faith that some other people have, but I strive to attain that in my life. Everyone has different talents and skills. My goal was to find what worked best for me.

I ended up becoming friends with a guy named Pastor Phil. He was the pastor who ran the ministry my dad was into called Set Free. It was primarily made up of biker dudes with tattoos who were into the street way of life. Most of the members called Phil "Chief" so I did too. Chief was a rough-looking dude with a shaved head and tattoos all over his neck and arms. He spent some time in prison and had turned his life around by finding the Lord. I started hanging out with the Set Free group for about a year or so.

Pastor Phil and I got really tight. I liked that the people in Set Free didn't refer to themselves as a ministry so much as they considered themselves to be a gang. I liked the idea of being associated with a gang better than a church. Even though the guys were gentle they still had a thug mentality that dismissed what other people thought of their style and

Me and Chief.

beliefs. I liked hanging out with Chief, learning about the Bible and the Christian way of life.

Chief wasn't your typical pastor. He always wore street clothes, liked to go out with the gang, ride his motorcycle, go to shooting ranges, and have good clean fun. I liked his style and approach. He wasn't what I perceived as being religious—he was just into God's word. That vibe worked well for me. In fact, I was so inspired by Chief that I decided to start studying to become a pastor. I got all the way through the Book of Matthew in my studies. When Jonathan found out I wanted to become a pastor, he thought it was great. He said we could claim the Korn studio as a church and get all sorts of tax write-offs. Of course, he was joking, but I was very serious in my pursuit.

Though we were pretty tight for a year or so after Dad died, Chief and I lost touch over the past couple of years. I got busy with Korn and he pursued other interests as well. When we drifted apart, I temporarily backed off from becoming a pastor. I would still like to finish my studies so I can some-day officiate at my children's weddings. I haven't pursued the pastor thing further but I still read the Bible every single day because the personal benefits are so great.

My new knowledge really helped me mend my relation-ships, especially with Dena. Even though she had agreed to marry me, we still had a lot of work to do to rebuild the loss of trust in our relationship. I started referring back to the Bible to help both of us understand the reasons I did the things I did. I could look up any word—from hate, love, or confusion—and show her what the Bible said about those emotions. It gave us a common ground to talk about her feelings and seek out the answers we would need to make it as a couple.

Even though we were communicating, Dena actually had a hard time accepting the new me. I was not the same man she fell in love with and she wasn't ready to give up her party life-style. I understood her resistance because she was so young. I had already lived a pretty full life and wanted something different.

I think it's basic human nature to doubt other people and their intentions. I know that people doubted mine when I finally got sober and discovered my faith. No one, not one single person, immediately accepted the new me as being genuine or sincere. That was tough to accept, but I knew my heart was pure so I didn't put any value in those opinions. No one had the power to dissuade me or knock me off the track because I didn't give them that control.

From my perspective, I was on my way to becoming a

much better version of myself. But that isn't quite how Dena saw things. She felt insecure from my past and doubtful of my commitment to being sober and faithful. It took a long time to slowly build back the trust I had destroyed, but we eventually worked through it. I was adamant about the reasons for my changes. I kept telling Dena what I'd said from the outset—that it wasn't for her, that I changed because I feared the Lord. I didn't fear Dena. I feared losing her, but I wasn't afraid of her. I had come to fear God, though. That was enough to keep me on the straight and narrow.

The stronger my faith got, the better our relationship became. I was no longer afraid of love. For most of my life, love was an uptight, angry, wrong-tone-of-voice, screaming, yelling, without-peace love. There were always arguments, cheating, alcohol, and drugs. It was a different type of love than I have come to know with Dena since I got sober and found the Lord. I have found peace, something I deeply cherish. I like the way it makes me feel. I can enjoy an evening at home with friends and family, where everyone is laughing, having a good time and where people aren't screaming and yelling at each other. I've wanted that my whole life. I didn't know you could have it.

About a year after I proposed, Dena and I finally tied the knot on May 13, 2006. I asked Chief to officiate over the ceremony. We got married at the St. Regis Hotel in Dana Point, California. The property is beautiful, with breathtaking sweeping views of the Pacific Ocean. I had a custom-made chocolate brown tux made from a guy Munky recommended. The tux was really cool with a brown bandana print vest underneath and we wore brown Converse Chucks. I had my hair in four braids with a matching brown bandana and beanie on my head. It was very rock-and-roll gangster.

On the day of our wedding, I had Chief and a few of the guys I'd gotten tight with from the gang come to my house to get ready for the ceremony. Eight black motorcycles rumbled up my driveway.

A friend loaned me his Bentley, and Chief and I drove to the hotel flanked by the eight Harleys. When we pulled up to the hotel, we must have looked like a fierce foreign dignitary with a funky police escort. When I got out of the car, I told all the guys to walk very slowly through the hotel. I wanted to take in every moment as we strolled through this very fancy lobby looking like we might rob the place and take hostages.

Me and Dena sealing it with a kiss.

No one made eye contact as we made our way through. I could see hotel guests lower their heads, afraid for their lives. It was kind of funny.

I remember standing at the altar thinking, *I'm really getting married.* In my heart, I knew I was finally doing it right. When Chief asked me if I would take Dena to be my wife, I said, "I 100 percent, with all my heart, commit my life to you. I do!" And that is how I really felt. I had fallen short on love and marriage so many times in the past, but this time I realized I was taking more than a vow of love, it was a vow of commitment. Everything inside me knew I was in the relationship for the long haul.

When Chief pronounced us husband and wife, I had a feeling of complete and utter happiness. In my heart, I would be with Dena for the rest of my life. As we turned and faced the crowd for the first time as husband and wife, for whatever reason, all I could think about was how much I wanted to have a baby together. It wasn't about the sex. It was about creating something that would be an extension of the two of us, our love and commitment and hope for our future.

We really enjoyed the reception. We entered the ballroom of the hotel to Mötley Crüe's "Too Young to Fall in Love." There were two oversized velvet chairs waiting for us that looked like they were for a king and queen, where we held court for hours. It was so much fun yet, still, all I wanted to do was get out of there to make love with my wife and make a baby.

At the end of the night, Dena and I made our way to our honeymoon suite. She surprised me by having rose petals strewn all over the room that was only lit by soft candlelight. We took a warm bath together before we fell into bed. When we began to make love, I knew our souls had connected in a different way than ever before. It was truly as if we had become one. As I let loose all my little guys, I was positive we conceived—not just a child, but our son.

We had planned to honeymoon in Prague but ended up canceling it at the last minute because I was tired of traveling so far away from home. Instead, we did a long weekend in Vegas where we enjoyed each other's company. Neither of us are big gamblers so we mostly spent our time relaxing in the sun and going to dinner and shows at night. A few weeks after our

Even though I was overjoyed, I still tried to look cool.

wedding, Dena went to the doctor who confirmed that we were in fact, expecting. We were overjoyed with our good news.

Even though I've gone through some really hard times, I now understand that those challenging times can actually help a relationship grow stronger. Once I learned to control my temper, arguments with Dena were very different. I was no longer short fused and quick to lash out. Looking back, so many of our fights were dumb, but they were fueled by the toxins I was feeding my body. Recently, Dena and I got into the first argument we've had in a long time. She was sitting

Getting a tattoo in my armpit. It was the most painful I've ever gotten.

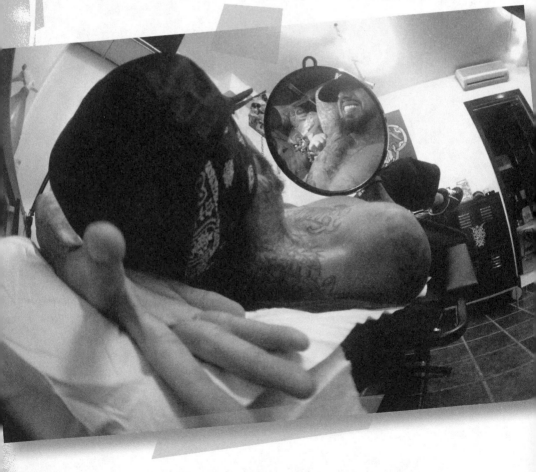

on the kitchen counter, swinging her legs back and forth and accidentally nailed me in the crotch—really hard. My initial reaction was one of rage. If I had been drunk with that rage, things would have turned out violent. I would have grabbed her by the hair and dragged her across the floor until she cried. Because I was sober, I could make the distinction that she didn't mean to hurt me. Whenever I feel any type of anger now, it's controlled. I think we all have triggers that cause us to behave in an angry way. Even Jesus had them.

You can be Christian and still have anger and rage—but it has to be controlled. Learning that about Jesus inspired me to strive for the same response when faced with dealing with my own emotions. In the end, Dena and I ended up laughing off the kitchen incident with no serious impact, except of course, the pain between my legs.

It's kind of funny when Dena and I talk about how things were when I was drinking and getting high. She always tells me that I was a totally different guy, saying I even looked different. It's true that since I got sober and started working out, I have lost thirty pounds. But Dena swears it isn't just the weight she has noticed. My eyes are clearer and my face is no longer bloated. She refers to the old me as her "ex-boyfriend." And I'm okay with that because I like the man I have become so much better. It's as if the real me has been set free.

Dena and I still have disagreements from time to time. But we have both learned not to hold on to our anger for too long. She has always been better at forgiving than me, but lately I seem to be right by her side if something goes down between us. Even though she doesn't get jealous like she used to, those old hurt feelings can rear their head from time to time. When they do surface, it no longer turns into World War III because neither one of us wants to fuel that fire. It's not worth the fight because there is no chance that I would ever go back to that way of life. Learning to pick your battles is the key to the success of every relationship.

I look around today and see all sorts of relationships around me where I know those two people love each other, but they're in a living hell. They bicker, fight, and talk down to each other, which makes it hard to let love shine through. I know that story firsthand. I used to live that way. When I figured out there was a choice to live a calmer, more peaceful life of love, I no longer wanted to live in hell. I much prefer living in my earthly heaven.

All you've got to do to experience a taste of what I have is to choose to live on the other side. It's the good dog–bad dog syndrome. It sounds a lot harder than it is. I've been there. I can tell you that it is really as simple as becoming aware of your actions. But just because change is a simple choice doesn't mean it's not hard work.

Ironically, after years of not appreciating school, I finally found a passion for doing homework. I like to take each part I read in the Bible daily and try to figure out how that particular passage fits into my current life. Sometimes I'll write about whatever I just read. For example, when I read Matthew 16:24–25, which says, "Then Jesus said to his disciples, 'If any of you want to be my follower, you must turn from your selfish ways. Take up your cross and follow me. If you try to hang onto your life you will lose it. But, if you give up your life for my sake, you will save it."

I always attempt to put my thoughts into more accessible words and take a more street approach because it helps the teachings make more sense to me. I think that approach is what made Chief so appealing to me. So my interpretation of the above scripture is what follows here:

To follow Christ is like if Jesus was a box of chocolate cake and He left the recipe to life on the back of the box. If you follow the recipe, you'll make a perfect cake every time. But if you make up your own recipe, you will never bake a perfect cake.

You can let everybody eat your chocolate cake, but what good is the cake if you never show anyone the box and how to follow the recipe?

If the owner of the box came to you and said, "Did you let anyone eat my cake?" you can say, "Yes."

And if the owner says, "Did you show them the box and tell them how to follow each step?" you can say, "Yes."

How happy do you think the owner of that recipe would be? Some people will burn the same chocolate cake over and over again for the rest of their lives and never get the recipe right. But what if right before you die, the owner of that recipe comes to you and says he can show you the way to make his perfect cake?

"All you had to do was flip the box over and follow the directions."

The answer was always there.

It took my wife a year or so after I gave up alcohol and drugs to make the same decision for herself. Dena always had strong faith so my beliefs were never an issue between us, but I had grown quite concerned about her drug use. She never had a drinking problem but she had become addicted to uppers. I finally had to give her an ultimatum to quit taking speed pills or she had to leave. I didn't threaten her as a way to get her to quit. I just couldn't take seeing her all jacked up. It felt wrong. I don't think getting sober was a difficult decision for her because she pretty much quit taking the pills cold turkey and, shortly thereafter, gave up drinking and smoking weed, too. She might occasionally have a drink or two with her girlfriends, but she no longer has a need to party. I'd like to think my newfound lifestyle influenced her to give up her own habits, but it doesn't really matter how she got there.

We believe that husbands and wives represent each other. Neither of us want other people to think our commitment isn't authentic. And, though I feel very strong in my personal commitment to my sobriety, there is always a chance that I could backslide into my old ways. I am human, and it would be untruthful to say I couldn't be tempted to have a drink or a rip off a bong. The key for me is staying focused and committed to feeding the good dog.

Making that decision isn't easy for a lot of people. I would love to have a relationship with my buddy Ham who chose to move out of my house after I changed my life. It was pretty obvious that he didn't want to change with me. And that's okay because I can't make anyone change who doesn't really want it for themselves. No one can. That's so important to understand if you love someone who is an addict. They're not behaving in a certain way to lash out at you. In fact, it has nothing to do with you or anyone else. It's their problem. Plain and simple.

When a friendship is destroyed, it is almost impossible to repair. Unless that person is around all the time and having them in your life really matters, I don't think you can ever fully recover from the damage that has been done. I learned to accept that people will come and go in life. Your real friends are the ones who really matter. I began to put my focus on salvaging and nurturing those relationships so they could get to know me after getting sober. I had spent twenty years destroying those relationships. I now had the daunting task of repairing them, which I knew was going to be a slow process—if they were salvageable at all.

The loss of Ham's friendship makes me sad because we were really tight, and now we don't talk. He works for Munky now and was recently on tour with us. We were cordial but far from the buds we once were. After he moved out, we text messaged for a while. I was trying to help him out with some advice on life, but he wanted no part of my insights.

If you're living a life of addiction, you go to bed with a bunch of regrets. I know how hard it is to get those thoughts to stop racing through your mind. I had so many sleepless nights, unaware that it was my conscience keeping me awake. I'd drown out the negative thoughts by taking a sleeping pill or having a couple of drinks before I went to bed, but it never made them disappear.

I know there are a lot of people who live in that same cycle, doing whatever it takes to sleep at night. Life comes at us fast. It's easy to get through the day when you have meetings, appointments, whatever. The great equalizer for all of us comes at nighttime. I think we are all the same when we lay our head down. Everybody does it. You, me, we're the same in that we all face our demons, our conscience, our regret, our guilt and remorse at night. You can't run from your mind. You can try to subdue the racing thoughts, but they are still there waiting for you when your buzz wears off. I know this better than most.

The secret to going to bed in peace is to make it through your day without any regrets. Yeah, I know. It's easier said than done. But, once you've found peace in your daily life, it's not as hard as you might think. I go to bed every night without the TV on and with a smile on my face because my conscience is clean. A clean conscience is the best drug in the world. The only way to get there is to stop lying, cheating, and hurting loved ones by acting wrong. It is the best feeling I have ever known. I wouldn't replace it with any drug—and I've tried them all. As I've said before, if getting stoned or taking pills were a better way to sleep every night, I'd be doing it.

To me, the meaning of true friendship is someone who tells you the truth no matter what—even if you don't want to hear what that person has to say. Let's face it; no one wants to hear their shortcomings. It's a hard pill to swallow, to listen to a friend lay the hard truth on the line. But, if you're good enough friends, you will understand that the other person is simply trying to help make your life better. You have no obligation to agree with what they're saying. But true friends will listen. And, if you're being completely honest with yourself, you will find that what your friend is saying is probably in your best interest and worth accepting, even if it hurts in the moment.

Don't get me wrong. I went through a lot to get here. It wasn't easy apologizing to every person I ever hurt. It took courage to ask for their forgiveness and lots of time for me to actually learn to forgive myself. Once I started living in my truth, I realized Jesus died for our sins, which meant He would forgive me for all of the rotten things I had done. That made self-forgiveness a little easier for me.

Once I had my life on the right path, it was time to get back to what I love doing most—music. Korn spent most of 2006 touring all over the world. We kicked off the See You on the Other Side Tour in early February, first touring the United States, and then heading to Asia and Australia before unexpectedly finishing in Europe, when Jonathan developed a rare blood disorder, after having a cyst removed, forcing us to cancel the rest of the planned dates. He was treated with a noninvasive, minor procedure, but complications occurred afterward when the doctors gave him the same antibiotic Dad took to help with his recovery. It had a negative effect on Jonathan, practically killing him. We had to cancel the rest of the tour so Jonathan could recover. I was scared I might lose him. I didn't want him to know I thought the whole situation was messed up, so I acted positive, telling him he'd be fine, but deep down, I was petrified he might die. By now you know that we're family. I've always felt a different kind of bond with Jonathan than the other guys in the band—after all, we literally grew up together. Now that I was sober, being around Jon was like finding my long-lost brother. We were getting to know each other all over again. Losing Dad was hard enough. I didn't want to lose Jonathan, too.

Luckily, Jon finally got the right treatment and was able to recover and get back on his feet. As soon as he was feeling up to it, we hit the road again in late July to kick off our annual Family Values Tour, which featured the Deftones, Stone Sour, Flyleaf, 10 Years, and Dir En Grey. By the time we played our last show of that tour in late September, everyone was exhausted. It had been a long, hard year. Even so, we wanted to jump right into the studio to start writing and recording. It didn't come as a big surprise to me when David announced he wasn't feeling ready to start the grueling process all over again. He said he wanted to take a break. I think he was simply burned out.

At the time, he was focused on running his steakhouse and opening a chain of bar and grills. He came to us and said he wanted to take a little time off to put his time and energy into pursuing the restaurants. We were all supportive and encouraged him to do whatever he needed to do. We told him we still planned to get back into the studio and record and to take as much time as he needed.

So, in December 2006, Korn announced that our second original member, David Silveria, would be going on hiatus. Jonathan made it official when he was asked about David's leaving on a Swedish radio station. When the DJ asked if David would be on our next album, Jon simply said, "I don' know, probably not." And that was that. David was gone.

Even though David and I played in a band together since we were in L.A.P.D., we never really talked. I never called him or made an effort to be his friend. I can't say we ever talked on the phone all these years, either. Even so, I always wanted the dude to be happy. I know there were lots of times in the past where I really hurt David. It was pretty clear that no matter what I said or did, we were never going to be friends. I wish things were different because I am such a different man today. Even so, I wish David well and hope that he finds true happiness in his life.

One of the most interesting aspects of getting sober for me came with the realization that Korn was now a sober band. Jonathan was the first to kick his habits. He was one of my greatest inspirations to find that kind of peace in my life. And even though we aren't all close friends, since Head and David have left the band, we've become a tight circle, tighter than we've ever been. We still have a good time together, but now it's sober fun. We make amazing kick-ass records, hang out and laugh all the time, only today we do it without slowly killing ourselves. And I think we are all better musicians now because we're focused and even more determined to make great music.

People have this false perception that they're really focused when they're stoned or wasted, but they are usually a big fat mess. I know. I've been there. For a musician, the true test comes when someone asks if you can play that same riff sober. I want to surround myself with people who have that light, that aura. There's no room for the darkness anymore.

CHAPTER 9

HERE TO STAY

By now you know that I used to be a slave to the dark side of life. I ran after it, literally chasing parties, drugs, alcohol, and women. It was a lot of work to live that way, and the consequences were literally killing me. I woke up shaking, spent my days vomiting, and couldn't sleep at night. I didn't care because I thought that was the only way to have fun. Once I changed my life, I realized I had to take all of that energy and persistence and put it toward something constructive, so I became a slave to the other side. I gave all of my attention to doing things that were good for me, such as cultivating healthy relationships, and I began working out all the time. Hitting the gym every day was hard work, but it made me feel good instead of bad. The results were so rewarding and much more gratifying.

Let's be honest. It's easy to crack open a beer and throw back a six-pack or more, but the results the next morning suck. For me, it usually became an open invitation to cheat,

Dena and I posing with the author of life on Korn's Salt Lake City tour stop.

overeat, or mouth off. It's a lot harder for me to get up and go to the gym for an hour and a half every single day, but I feel better about myself and know that I am not hurting anyone else by making that choice.

In less than two hours' time, I could do something good and feel great the rest of the day. Before too long, though, that high from working out wasn't enough. I wanted to keep doing things that made me feel that way all day long.

Something as simple as showing a stranger kindness began to make me feel really good. I was recently on a U.S. tour where I spent the bulk of my free time during the days walking around getting to know the sights and vibe of the various cities we were in. I often came across homeless people on the street. I always stopped to talk for a while. I liked hearing their stories and perspectives. One particular time a guy came running up behind me. He scared me at first, but then I realized he recognized me and just wanted to say hi. He had dirt all over his face, his hair was all matted and knotted up, and most of his teeth were missing. Everything about this guy screamed he was homeless.

We began to walk together while he started to tell me his story. He'd just gotten out of prison after serving fifteen years (he never told me why). He'd been on the street for a couple of months. He said his good buddy from inside the joint had written some lyrics to a song, and he wanted to know if he could read them to me.

"Yeah, man, go ahead." I never stopped walking.

I don't recall what the song was about, but I remember the lyrics were really dark. After he finished reading them to me, he paused before revealing that his friend had recently committed suicide. I felt bad but understood there are people in this world who will never beat down their demons. I didn't say much. I just listened. We walked a few more blocks until he pointed out another buddy on the street corner across from us. He told me how he played the buckets like drums for money. The guy was trying every angle to connect with me on music. Finally he asked if he and his friend could come to our concert.

"Sure," I said. "Let's find a piece of paper so you can give me your name and I'd be happy to put you on my guest list." I was being sincere. I wanted to hook these guys up, for no other reason than they were fans and deserved to have a good time. As the dude wrote his information down, I stopped him, looked him square in the eyes, and said, "What do you think I'm all about?"

"I believe in Jesus." That was his answer. It was freaky and weird. Where did that come from? There wasn't a single moment where I mentioned God or Jesus while we talked. But much like Dad had treated me over the years, I looked at him with complete love and wasn't being judgmental. It was pretty heavy to realize that something so simple meant so much to both of us. I told him he made my day and then said good-bye.

Someone once told me that "you can never try to force other people to accept Christ. See to it that they are so favorably impressed by your own life and your conduct and the peace and joy that you radiate that they will come running to you of their own accord, begging you to give them the wonderful thing that you have." Man, this guy on the street was walking proof of how powerful faith and belief in the Lord can be. When you're living a real life full of unconditional love and peace, people will want what you have. You don't have to go to them and say, "Do you know what you need?" It doesn't work that way. People will turn their backs on you before you can get the next words out of your mouth. I should know because that is exactly what I did for years. No one wants to be told what to do. When you live a positive life, doing good things for other people, the consequences are rewarding. Why not choose to make your soul happier by doing good deeds rather than by regretting things?

Look, there are plenty of days I make mistakes. If something happens that wasn't between another person and me, I pray to God and ask for His forgiveness and help to get through my daily challenges. But, if I get into an argument with someone or say something that isn't right, I always make sure I settle things before I go to bed at night. I make it a point to never go to bed angry. Once I apologize, it is up to the other person to decide if they are going to forgive me. If they do, then all is good. If not, the burden is now on them.

Remember this: the probable reason they won't forgive you is because of their pride. They are going to suffer for their pride because it impacts everything. That is why it is so important to not let yours get in the way. Even when I know I am right, I apologize because it defuses a potentially explosive situation. A lot of people can't do that, but I have found that the fallout from being prideful is far worse than the benefits. If you let pride interfere in your relationships, sooner or later you will discover you're pretty lonely.

I never knew how lonely I was until I got sober. Once I had some clarity, I could take a step back and ask myself some pretty hard questions about the other people in my life. Were these my friends or were they just hanging out to party with me? It didn't take me very long to figure out that many of the people I saw were just hanging on. My sobriety intimidated them, so many stopped coming around. They weren't ready to face their demons, and I wasn't about to tag along while they figured things out.

I am not perfect, but I am doing the best I can, and that is all anyone can hope for. I'm definitely a work in progress, but I finally have the peace I've been searching for. I sometimes look around and notice that some people I know are trying to find peace and might even make you think they are at peace, but the truth is, they don't have it on the inside. They've given up their obvious addictions but traded them in for others. Some gave up drinking but started smoking cigarettes nonstop. I've never been to an AA meeting, but I know many of the people who go are coffee and cigarette fiends. I'm not saying that's a bad thing—it's definitely a lot better than continuing to use drugs and alcohol, but I don't think they're really at peace. To truly get clean, you have to come clean.

Holding secrets in can kill you. I know everyone has experienced how good it feels to get something they've been holding on to off their chest. Forgiveness begins with saying what you've got to say, putting it out there, and then letting it go. Don't kill yourself for someone else's sake. Say what you've got to say and move on. If people are your good friends, you can tell them the truth. If they're not, you're better off without them anyway. Coming clean is the perfect test of any relationship.

It wasn't easy confessing all of my sins to Dena, but we worked through it and became much stronger as a couple because I wasn't afraid to speak the truth. I was willing to lose her. I didn't want to. I hoped I wouldn't, but I was willing to risk the greatest love of my life for the peace I felt after my confession. I never dreamed our life could get better than it was after we got married, but it did.

After our wedding, my relationship with Dena was in a much stronger place than it had ever been. We were both sober, happy, and living the life. After we found out she was pregnant with our son, I knew I wanted to do so many things different this time around. It was important to me to become the dad I never could be to my daughters. I thank God every day they were too young to remember all of the negative consequences of my absence and addictions. Thankfully, my son would never know the old Fieldy, so I wouldn't have to make up for lost time with him.

Dena's pregnancy brought out a strong need inside my heart to finally become a good dad to Sarina, who was then ten, and Olivia, nine. Spending time with them has been so much better since I got sober. With the impending arrival of my son, quality time with the girls became a priority.

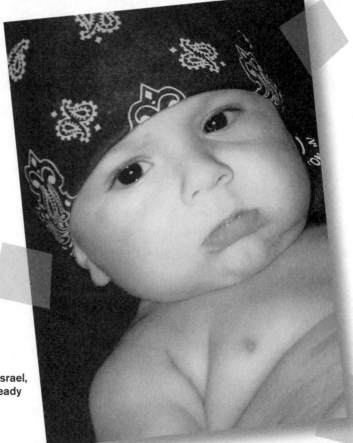

My son, Israel, getting ready to rock.

Even though I don't have much of a relationship with their mother, Dena and Shela have become quite good friends. That makes things a lot easier for everyone. I never try to interfere with the way Shela is raising our girls because she is really the primary caregiver. They're both honor roll students, are really respectable, and are very cool kids. Clearly, she is doing a good job, so why should I get on her case if there's something I don't agree with? That's called picking your battles, something I have definitely learned to do, which has made life a lot easier for all of us.

I get to see my daughters every other weekend when I am not on tour. Instead of sleeping all the time like I used to, I now look forward to the time we have together as a family. I get them ready for bed every night, making sure they brush their teeth, put their pajamas on, and settle in for a good night's sleep. They usually crawl into bed and watch television for a few minutes before I turn it off and tell them "it's time to talk." I'll spend an hour listening to each tell me all about their day. I ask about school, how they're doing, and if there's anything they want to talk about. Before I tuck them in, the three of us will pray together.

Man, it is so pure when a kid prays. They pray to God and ask Him to help all of the hungry people in the world and to cure the sick. They'll ask God to help all the families we know to get along. It touches my heart every time. Praying with my children has become one of the most cherished moments, because they open up on a different level than they do the rest of the day. One hour of talk time more than makes up for a busy day filled with activities. All of the pretenses are gone. Our guards are down and we are at ease with one another. I don't have to be the disciplinarian and they can just be kids. It's beautiful.

I now make time to take the girls to the park. I'll run while they Rollerblade or ride their bikes. They can't believe that I can run so many laps without stopping because it wasn't so long ago that I couldn't run a single lap. The idea of having fun in the park was so foreign to me. I've learned to have fun during the day because there is nothing but trouble and temptation at night. These days, nighttime is meant for sleeping. Anything else is a waste of time.

Now, when I finish running, we'll toss a Frisbee together, play, and laugh. Just being active with Sarina and Olivia is so much more than I could offer a few years ago. I used to just go through the motions. I'd take them to the park, put on my Walkman, and sit on a bench because I was too hungover to participate. Sometimes I'd bring a couple of beers to take the edge off and start that vicious cycle all over again. Thank God those days are over.

I think my daughters always knew their dad was a rock star, but it now seems to be sinking in that I'm very different from most of the other dads. They've both been on tour with me a number of times, but I don't think they ever understood what it was all about. I plan to take them on our next U.S. tour for a week or two and let them hang out with their pops. I want them to see what I do. And I can finally feel comfortable enough with them being on the road and not fear they'll be exposed to things that would be outrageously inappropriate, things they would have surely seen in the past.

Since getting sober I've made a conscious effort to shield my daughters from the bad influences that could impact their lives. There's no drinking or smoking around them, no cussing or wrong tone of voice. I go out of my way to show my girls a better way to live by setting an example through my own actions. If you left all decisions up to kids, they'd do whatever

With my kids, Sarina, Israel, and Olivia, celebrating my birthday. They're the only presents I need.

they want. They'd eat chocolate cake and drink soda all day long because they don't know any better. I grew up watching my parents drink alcohol while telling me not to. You know what? All that did was make me want to steal beer from them. Parents have a responsibility to teach their children the right choices through their own actions. I can't say Mom and Dad didn't try with me—I'm sure they did—but I wasn't the type of kid who was going to listen. I had to find my own way—on my own time. My daughters see how I live, and they know I'm living my life by following my heart.

I don't want my children to go through the depths of hell to discover there's a better way, but I know they will come around to formulating their own beliefs someday. Between their mom's faith and mine, they've had some very good role models to follow, if that is what they choose in the future.

I simply want them to have the right tools to make the best choices when the time comes. Those lessons have to start young. I've become a pretty strict disciplinarian. When they're in a "time-out," I make sure they use that time wisely. I'll set the timer on my stove for forty-five minutes and tell them they can read a book or sit quietly to think about what they did wrong. I used to be a pushover, but not anymore. When my daughters ask me if they can have soda, I say no, and explain to them why drinking water is healthier for them. The upshot is they see me eating healthy, too, so there's no double standard. They can't say, "Well, you eat cake, why can't we?" They see me snacking on apples and drinking lots of water all day long. I can't even imagine how I'd feel if they had been aware of my drinking or, worse, my drug use. It was by the grace of God that I got sober before they tuned into those habits instead of my healthier new way of life. Knowing I genuinely live a certain way makes it easier for me to be a good role model.

I keep close tabs on what's happening inside my home these days. Dena and I have a lot of family and friends who come over or stay with us. They all know I can only have positive energy in the house. Having everyone on the same page makes it easier to create an atmosphere where no one is at another's throat, arguing, cussing, or saying cutting things. I haven't told anyone what to do or how to act. I just let them watch me live. It's contagious.

Even though Dena and I had been together for several years, I had never met her dad, Rick. They were estranged for most of her life. He was living in Riverside, which was a pretty far drive from Laguna, so we never had a reason to cross paths. I was working on the Stillwell project with my good friend Q-Unique, who had previously been the front man for the Arsonists when I received a frantic call from Dena's stepmom, Alma, saying her husband was in trouble. Q, who is from Brooklyn, had flown out to Los Angeles to meet with me for the first time a couple of days earlier. We were in the middle of laying down a hot track with four of his homies when I got the call.

Rick had a long history of drug abuse. Alma told me he was missing and suspected he was out on a binge. She was worried he might end up in jail if I didn't come out to the house and find him. I could hear the panic in her voice. She was genuinely scared for his life. I am sure there were times in my life where others had that same tone of voice, worrying about me.

Even though I was in the middle of a recording session, I had to help. I barely knew Q and hoped that he would understand. It wasn't very professional, but a time comes when your family has to take a priority over work. And even though I didn't know Rick, he was my wife's dad. I had no choice. I had to go. I reassured Q that he and his crew could stay and continue recording, that it was all good. I think he was kind of tripping out but seemed to understand.

Dena and her sister Kristy went with me for the ride. When we got to the house, Rick was still missing so we sat and waited, hopeful that he would eventually come home. When he finally walked through the door, he looked at his two daughters and got very nervous. He didn't know what to do. He certainly knew who I was but had no idea what I was all about. I stood up, introduced myself, and said, "Come talk to me in the backyard."

We went outside where we talked for a few minutes. I don't think he knew what to expect. I came at him with nothing but love. I asked Rick if he wanted to come back to Laguna with us for a while. I told him he could stay in our home for as long as he needed to so that he could get healthy. He was looking really thin. He was probably around 140 pounds when he should have been closer to 180. He looked like death was knocking on his door. It hadn't been that long since I lost Dad. I didn't want Dena to suffer the same pain and loss. Thankfully, Rick didn't put up a fight. He agreed to come with us.

I spent the next several days talking to him about how I got my life together and the steps I had to take to change my life. I gave him my whole story. I talked about being set free and the journey to get there. He knew from talking with me that I was being honest and sincere. I had lived a rough life—I'm sure rougher than he expected. After days of confessing to each other, Rick finally told me he didn't want to die.

"If I am going to do this, Fieldy, it's going to have to be with someone who has been there, someone who truly needed to change as much as I need to."

I was the right guy. I assured Rick that I would be there for him until he could pull his life together. We told each other stories for days, like we were two soldiers swapping old war tales of all the dumb things we had done in the past and our path to survive. Just talking about the dark times helped Rick see that there was still a chance for a future. We bonded through those weeks. There are a lot of qualities about Rick that I truly admire. I am happy to say that even though he isn't quite to the point in his life where I am, he has gotten healthy and is now trying to walk on the right path. Every day is a struggle. When Rick falls, he doesn't let it set him back. He picks himself up and starts all over again. Even though he is fifteen years older than me, he now jokes that I am more like his dad than his son. He doesn't realize that I look up to him, too.

So many good things come from living a truly positive life.

God wants to bless us with overflowing abundance. We all deserve happiness and bliss. It's funny when I think about my home now. It's the same house I owned that, back in the day, I avoided going to. It was a large empty house. I didn't think there was anything there for me. It turns out, the house wasn't the problem. I had to create the vibe I was seeking. I found something far more fulfilling than money could ever buy. *Peace, serenity, and sobriety.*

Dena and I welcomed my first son, Israel, on February 9, 2007. It is so exciting when I look at my boy. I cried the first time I held him in my arms. It was strange because I held him right after he was born. I was laughing and crying all at once. I had a baby boy. I couldn't believe how emotional I got. I have tremendous hope for his future, knowing I can raise him to become more successful than me. I plan to give him every opportunity to become a powerful man in this world.

The first year of his life went by so fast. Everyone tells you to brace yourself for how quickly time passes when you have kids. I didn't fully understand what that meant until Dena gave birth to our son. I wasn't around very much for Sarina and Olivia's baby years, so I didn't have a point of reference. It was so cool to watch Israel grow from this wobbly, flimsy thing that eats, poops, and naps all day long to becoming a strong, sturdy little boy. Being there for my son has truly been one of the great joys of my life. I can go to the park with him, someday play ball, and hopefully outrun him, at least for a while. I am looking forward to those experiences where I used to dread them.

I was on the 2008 Bitch We Have a Problem Tour in Europe when Israel turned one. I had to make a hard choice not to fly home to be there with him and Dena that day. Thankfully, in the world of computers and the Internet, I was able to watch him blow out his candles (with a little help from his mom) and could sing happy birthday to him from my hotel room six thousand miles away.

Life on the road is so different now. I did things on this last tour that were way out of the ordinary from past tours. For example, when we were traveling through France, I realized that the family of Sebastien, our band photographer, lived close to where we were scheduled to play. I knew he didn't get to see his family very often as he is usually on the road with us, so I suggested we detour on one of our days off to drop in on his mom and dad. His dad came to pick us up at the hotel where we were staying and drove us back to their home. He didn't speak a word of English, and I didn't speak French.

Their house was a typical French country home, with a garden in the back and a small yard overlooking the spectacular countryside. His parents welcomed me into their home like I was family. I felt so comfortable. His father made a variety of fresh crepes right on the grill. My favorite was the chocolate crepes. I watched closely as Sebastien's dad carefully drizzled chocolate on the inside of the homemade crepes, folding them and dusting each with a sprinkle of powdered sugar. They were delicious. I could have easily eaten a dozen. Even though we didn't speak the same language, I could tell his dad understood how much I enjoyed his cooking. Food is truly an international language.

I spent the rest of the afternoon looking at family photos as Sebastien translated for his family and me. I've known Sebastien for years but I never took the time to get to know him. His family was overwhelmed because they knew he has worked for the band but they had never met any of us. His father told Sebastien that he was so moved by the afternoon that he couldn't eat. He said he was being fed by his emotions and not the crepes.

Just before we left, a little boy who was about five years old came to the house. I was really missing my kids so I asked Sebastien to call him over.

I looked at the little boy with as serious a face as I could and said, "J'du sui alla petit zsa zsa moo shoo." It was nothing but gibberish. I thought I was being funny. The little boy looked confused. He muttered something to Sebastien and took off.

When I asked what he said, Sebastien responded, "I don't know shit about what that guy is saying!"

That was a really great day. I had never taken took the time to stop and appreciate the people around me who made life on the road tolerable or who really care about Korn and its members. I spent more time with Jon and Munky than ever before. Life on the road is so much better than it ever was.

Being on this last tour was really different from any other I can recall. The tour was originally called the Bitch We Got a Problem Tour until Jimmy Bryant, one of our managers who works with Jeff and Pete, decided to correct the grammar. All of the promotional material went to print with the word *have* instead of *got* so it just stayed the way it was. To be fair, Jimmy did come to us and ask if he could exchange the two words. I guess none of us were listening carefully enough because we gave him the go-ahead. He kept telling us how cool "Bitch We Have a Problem" would look on T-shirts and hats. We were down with the idea. It didn't occur to any of us that the single was titled "Bitch We Got a Problem" until it was too late.

Tour names aren't really all that important. For the most part, it's all about marketing. It was only after we received our tour books that we realized what had happened. It made Jon, Munky, and me laugh. We ended up doing two European tours, South America, South Africa, Australia, New Zealand, and Mexico using the wrong name.

Jimmy is a really good guy. We all love working with him, but we wouldn't want to get directions from the dude. One time we were in New York doing a record signing for what seemed to be several hours. When we sign, we will generally stay until the very last autograph has been done. We never leave anyone out (unless the police ask us to leave!). When it came time to leave the signing, Jimmy headed toward a door that we all knew led to the bathrooms and not the exit. None of us followed him because he always goes the wrong way. If Jimmy tells us to turn right, we're going left. We all laughed as Jimmy split in one direction and we headed in the other, looking over our shoulders to see how long it would take him to figure it out.

Touring Africa was one of the great highlights of my career. We stayed at the Westcliff, a really amazing hotel in Johannesburg. We were in South Africa for a week and a half to play two shows, one in Johannesburg and the other in Cape Town, so it was a minivacation for us. I asked Dena to come spend those ten days with me so we could make the most of it and spend some much needed and overdue time together. Dena usually joins me on the road for a week or two every month or so. Since we had the baby it's been a little more challenging for her to get away. I look forward to her joining up with me, now more than ever.

We had a cottage in front of the pool so we got to hang out and relax. We spent some time shopping, trying to take in the

African culture. Dena bought handmade bracelets and other knickknacks. We stopped in a local market to buy some water when we noticed two little kids, who couldn't have been older than three and five. They were there buying groceries. Something about that sight inexplicably touched both of us and reduced Dena and me to tears. They were so young to be out by themselves. I couldn't imagine my daughters doing that when they were that young.

In Cape Town, a bunch of us decided to get together to hike up Table Mountain. The mountain stands 3,563 feet above sea level. We had a choice of two routes to take. One was shorter and easier, and the other was steeper and longer. We chose the harder route. It took two hours to get to the top. I was gung ho from beginning to end, but most of the others had to take several breaks along the way. When we got to the summit, we were in awe of the beauty that surrounded us. I could see the ocean behind us and Cape Town to the front. It felt so good to accomplish something like hiking to the top of that mountain. In the old days I could have come to Africa and never experienced any of the beauty or culture. I look forward to touring now because it gives me the chance to experience new things and do stuff that is out of the ordinary for me. Now that I have a clear head I can appreciate the opportunity I have to see the great sites and wonders around the world. I now understand that it's not every day I get to climb a mountain in Africa. All we have is the moment, and if you don't seize that moment, you will never get that same chance again because it becomes the past.

We played our first show with Good Charlotte while they kicked off their 2008 world tour. I had met those guys before but I didn't really know them. When I ran into Benji Madden in the lobby of our hotel, he said he was there with his new girlfriend and asked if I wanted to hang out. I said, yes. He gave me his cell phone number so we could make plans. I told him to come see us backstage before the Johannesburg show. When he did, he walked in with a woman I recognized but couldn't really place. Dena immediately realized that Benji was with Paris Hilton. They were so shy at first. Thankfully, Dena and Paris hit it off, so we ended up hanging out a lot for the rest of the week. I couldn't believe how the press hounded Paris. It was crazy. I had no idea she was so famous. People were screaming at her like she was Michael Jackson while the rest of us stood around practically going unrecognized.

Benji and Paris told us about the safari they had gone on and said that Dena and I had to do the same before leaving Africa. Even though other people had told us it was a hassle to go, that it took five hours to get to the location and then another five hours back, Benji and Paris were so enthusiastic that we decided to take the chance. We booked our excursion the next day. The company we booked with guaranteed that we would see all sorts of wildlife, including lions, elephants, rhinos, buffalo, leopards, maybe even Bigfoot and King Kong. We were taken out in a big open-air Jeep so we could see everything without any obstruction. We drove for about an hour until we got to what looked like the middle of nowhere. We were served breakfast when we arrived and then cruised around in search of the animals.

I was stunned when we came upon our first sighting, a big gray elephant that was facing us head-on. I was tripping out at making eye contact with this beautiful wild animal. He flared his ears out and threw his trunk up as if to say, "I see you, too." Then, suddenly, he began to charge toward the Jeep. I was so caught up in the peacefulness of the moment that I didn't realize we could have been in any danger. We got out in the nick of time but the second Jeep that was behind us almost got rammed in the side. I could hear everyone screaming, but the elephant missed when he charged. Their giant Jeep looked like a Matchbox toy next to the stature of the African elephant.

I was so moved by the experience of being in the wild that I hope to someday return with my children to show them the wonder and beauty of Africa. I have taken my daughters to the zoo many times but the freedom of seeing animals in their natural environment is so different from seeing animals who are kept in captivity. There were no walls or boundaries to separate the animals from us. Everything was within reach.

After we left Africa, the band headed to Rio de Janeiro, Brazil, to play a show with Ozzy. I was really surprised to see how poverty-stricken the city was. We stayed at the world-famous Copacabana Hotel, which is in vast contradiction to the location where it resides. When we checked into the hotel, we were warned to be extra careful when walking the streets. Crime is a big problem, especially robberies of tourists. From the outside looking in, the streets looked like any other tourist area, loaded with T-shirt and souvenir shops, but the hotel was adamant that the area wasn't safe.

I told Dena that I needed to use the ATM machine. When we asked for directions, the nearest one was just a few blocks away.

The concierge said, "Go left out of the hotel. Walk two blocks and then turn right. It'll be right there."

Dena and I walked out the door, turned left and came to the first corner.

"I think we're supposed to turn right here," I said.

"No. He said to go two blocks. We need to walk straight for another block and then turn right." Dena was certain she was right.

We got into a disagreement over who was right and ended up walking back to the hotel.

I was so frustrated, I told Dena I wanted to go out alone for a while. I could see a giant statue of Jesus, known as Christ the Redeemer, atop the Corcovado Mountain, from the window of my hotel. The statue is now considered one of the New Seven Wonders of the World. Something was calling me to go to the top. I called my friend Sebastien to come with me so we could take some photos. He was thrilled to go. We boarded a train to get to the top where we met some tribal-looking guys who played the bongos to music from a boom box the whole trip up. They had no idea who I was so it was a lot of fun to just hang out and enjoy listening and dancing to their music.

When I got off the train, I ran into Zakk Wylde, Ozzy's guitarist. We said hello and talked for a minute until I said I had to go. As I made my way closer to the statue, I noticed a film crew shooting a cooking show. I stopped for a minute to check it out. I was determined to get on camera to plug the band. They let me do a cutaway on camera for fun, though I doubt they actually ended up using it.

The view from atop the mountain was spectacular. Like Africa, I could see the ocean and the entire city of Rio below. The statue is enormous. It is made of reinforced concrete and stands 130 feet high. Construction took nine years! The statue was hit by lightning a few months before I was there. Miraculously, while trees and debris fell down the mountain-side, there was no damage to the statue itself. I have to admit that I definitely felt the presence of God up there. It was so peaceful that I forgot all about my fight with Dena. I couldn't wait to get back down the mountain to tell her all about my afternoon.

When I got back to the hotel, I bumped into Ray, one of my favorite drummers I have ever played with. He told me he went down the street to use the ATM and was mugged at knifepoint. He said that a couple of guys came up behind him and demanded all of his money. Since he was on his way to the ATM, he didn't have any. When the muggers failed to get cash, they grabbed his gold necklace right off his body. They yanked it off in one pull. When they told Ray to hand over his iPhone, he refused. He threw a kick in the air that landed straight into the other guy's chest, sending him flying into the street. They took off running, afraid that Ray was going to come after them again. I don't know if I would have put up a fight over my cell phone. I would probably have said, "here you go." I thought about Ray's run-in for a minute and realized, that could have been Dena and me. I wasn't sure why we got into our fight earlier in the day, but now I know it was divine intervention.

So now you know all about me. I used to think I had a good life but I never knew what that really meant until now. There's a lot of opportunity in the world that is ours for the taking. What you choose to do with those prospects is completely up to you. Have the courage to live your dreams. Don't let other people stand in your way of finding real happiness and genuine peace. It's the greatest high I've ever known.

And now, with God's love and guidance, I can truly say, I've *Got the Life*.

10

MY DIARIES

While writing this book I came across several entries in my personal journals that inspired me along my journey. I wrote all of these after I got sober as a reminder to myself of where I've been and the path I'm on now. I thought I'd share a few of my favorites with you, with the hope that these thoughts will somehow inspire you to find your own trail that leads you to believe you've *Got the Life.*

A failed dream is better than a dream. Let me start with taking the word "can't" out of your vocabulary . . . and you can. I heard this saying, "You can do anything if you put your mind to it." But I have found that you need to put your mouth to it. You need to tell people your dreams. And not by saying, "I want to be a rock star." You have to say, "I am going to be a rock star."

Or whatever it is you're going to be. I'm the same as you. I just didn't say, "I want to be . . ." I said, "I'm going to be . . ." If your dream is to be an actor, doctor, or even the president, you have to tell people. Convince them that you are the best. Then, follow up. Even if you think you're bugging them, keep following up and then change. Keep following up until they change their number. If that happens, then find someone else to tell. Never give up.

"Keep on asking and you will receive what you asked for. Keep on seeking and you will find. Keep on knocking and a door will open to you. For everyone who asks, receives. Everyone who seeks, finds. And to everyone who knocks, the door will be open" Matthew 7:7–8.

If you put the time into your dreams, it won't matter how may hours you put in, it will never feel like work. If it does, it's not your dream. Keep seeking. When you have a job, you can't wait to clock out. But when you have a dream, the time that you give will be rewarding. Since 1992, when Korn was first signed to a record label, to this very day, I have not worked. The day I feel that I have to go to work is no longer a dream; it's a nightmare.

Have you ever heard the expression, "Live your life to the fullest"?

Don't waste your life. There are only so many hours in a day and you can never get those back. Don't waste hours of your life on the "sinnernet" or watching the news. You were made to make a difference.

When you're eating food, you have to be careful about what goes into your mouth or it could ruin your health. The same goes with what your eyes take in. If your eyes are watching the news, then you will begin to think negative thoughts, be depressed, and sad.

If you are addicted to the "sinnernet," then be careful about what you are looking at. You are putting poison into your brain.

Don't give up.

Write notes of things you've got to get done.

Never stop praying.

Nothing is too hard.

Stop wasting time and go take a walk so you can hear all of your good ideas. You cannot hear your soul talk to you if you have noise around you 24/7. There is one thing we all have in common; our inner soul—that deep-down inside spirit that tells you your dreams.

It's not what you say in life, it's how you say it. Most of us talk before we think. The mouth is the hardest thing to train and it is more deadly than a loaded gun. Proverbs 13:3 says, "Those who control the tongue will have a long life. Opening your mouth can ruin everything." When you try to make a change, it will feel fake at first and you will want to say, "This is not for me."

Don't believe it. Stick with it for a few months, and your new ways will become natural. All new habits feel unnatural at first. A lot of us are alone because of the carelessness of our words. This is one of the most important things you can change. It's never too late.

If you are going to say something to someone and you have to put your eyebrows down and push them together, you should not say a word and rethink what you're going to say. When someone makes me mad or I disagree with them, I will text them later with what I think or tell them to their face after I've thought about the situation. If you're in a conversation where you feel yourself getting mad, realize it is a trap and get out. Tell the other person you have to go to the bathroom— even if you don't—and leave.

Go someplace and pray. If you're on the phone, tell the other person you have to set the phone down for a minute—and pray. If you work on the words that come out of your mouth, your whole life will change.

Treat life as if you were Korn's number one fan, pushing your way to the front row. You're going to get elbowed in the face, but you don't stop and fight, because you want that number one spot. If you fall and get trampled by fans, you get up and push your way through. You're headed for the front row knowing that there is nothing that can stop you. You're in the middle of the mosh pit and it's like a human tornado with dudes swinging their arms, throwing punches and kicking out of control. You're scared and you have to go through it, so you get sucked into the pit and go around a few times. Now your clothes are ripped up, you've got a black eye, a bloody lip, and are drenched in sweat. You're almost there, but it doesn't look good. The fans are as tight as a can of sardines. You slip your sweaty body between the "children of the Korn." Now you can see the stage. Here comes a Korn fan running from the stage and like a swan, he dives into the crowd and lands on your face, breaking your nose. It still doesn't stop you, so you press forward just in time to hear your favorite song. You made it to the front row with an ear-to-ear smile, having the time of your life because you did it!

Hebrews 12:1 in the Bible says, "Therefore since we are surrounded by such a huge crowd of witnesses to the life of faith, let us strip off every weight that slows us down, especially the sin that so easily trips us up." Don't get caught up in the crowds of life. Keep pushing until you reach your goals.

If you owe an apology to someone, take a chance
and do it. Most likely the person will forgive you,
and if he doesn't, that wasn't your friend anyway.
Stop worrying if your friend will accept it. It takes
less time and energy to say you're sorry than it
does to worry every day about it.

There is nothing better or more exciting than
telling your friend "no." If my friend asks if I want
a beer, I say, "No, I don't drink." If he still wants
to hang out with me, then he's a true friend.

When it comes to saying yes, that's almost
never. If my friend says, "Do you want to go to
Vegas this weekend?" my first reaction is to say
yes. But the right answer for me is to say, "Let me
think about it and I'll get back to you tomorrow."

When you tell somebody yes, it ends up a mess.
Avoid the word "yes" until the next day or
at least for a few hours so you can think about
all of the possible pitfalls.

You can make new friends every day but they
aren't really your friends until you hurt them.
I've had a lot of roommates in my day and when
someone becomes your roommate, most of the
time he becomes a good friend. Several years ago,
my friend Ham became my roommate and my best
friend. We did everything together. I have yelled
at him, disrespected him, and almost got into a
fistfight or two along the way. I think I even

made him cry. We made up and he forgave me for all of the wrong I did over the years. That is a friend. When I stopped drinking, smoking pot, and chasing women, I lost my friend. He moved out of my house and we haven't spoken for more than three years.

I thought he was my friend, but he just wanted to party. When I tried to reach out and help him, Ham got so angry with me for interfering in his life. I wasn't trying to interfere—I was hoping to help.

You've probably heard the saying, "Friends come and go." I have found that I never truly lost friends. I will always forgive them no matter what they do to me. I will always be here when they're ready to come back around.

Never give up. Write down notes of all the things you've got to get done and then do them.

Never stop praying. Nothing is too hard. Give a stranger your time. Make a new friend.

Forgive everyone and stop lying.

ACKNOWLEDGMENTS

I'd like to thank Laura Morton for having patience with me during our exactly one hour conversations and for helping find other ways for saying the word *cool*. And to her assistant, Adam Mitchell, for helping Laura get my thoughts on the page.

To my wife, Dena, for helping me dig deep enough and for giving me the freedom to say all I needed to say.

To my dad, whose death saved my life. The life he lived helped inspire me to understand there's more to life than I once thought.

To my mom, who was always there for me and loved me no matter what.

To Sarina and Olivia—I am so proud of the people you've turned into. You get good grades, you're really sweet girls, and I am really proud of the life you're both living.

To Israel—you put inspiration into my life even though you're only a year and a half. You're my little boy and I can't wait to watch you grow up.

The Firm:

To Alan Nevins, Jimmy Bryant, Peter Katsis, and Jeff Kwatinetz.

Thank you for believing in me and always giving me the chance to make new dreams happen in my life.

Harper Collins:

Thanks to my awesome editor, Mauro DiPreta, his assistant, Jennifer Schulkind, as well as Lisa Gallagher, Lynn Grady, and Brianne Halverson for all of their hard work and belief in this project.